THE HISTORY & CULTURE of NATIVE AMERICANS

The Comanche

THE HISTORY & CULTURE of NATIVE AMERICANS

THE HISTORY & CULTURE of NATIVE AMERICANS

The Comanche

T. JENSEN LACEY

Series Editor
PAUL C. ROSIER

CHELSEA HOUSE
PUBLISHERS
An imprint of Infobase Publishing

Thanks to LaDonna Harris, Nick and Marion Mejia,
Patti Edmundson, and the staff of Comanche Nation News.
This book is dedicated to my husband Eric. TJL

The Comanche

Copyright © 2011 by Infobase Publishing

All rights reserved. No part of this book may be reproduced or utilized in any form or by any means, electronic or mechanical, including photocopying, recording, or by any information storage or retrieval systems, without permission in writing from the publisher. For information contact:

Chelsea House
An imprint of Infobase Publishing
132 West 31st Street
New York NY 10001

Library of Congress Cataloging-in-Publication Data

Lacey, Theresa Jensen.
  The Comanche / T. Jensen Lacey.
    p. cm. — (The history and culture of Native Americans)
  Includes bibliographical references and index.
  ISBN 978-1-60413-789-7 (hardcover)
  1. Comanche Indians—History—Juvenile literature.   2. Comanche Indians—Social life and customs—Juvenile literature.   I. Title.   II. Series.
  E99.C85L33 2011
  978.004'974572—dc22   2010016113

Chelsea House books are available at special discounts when purchased in bulk quantities for businesses, associations, institutions, or sales promotions. Please call our Special Sales Department in New York at (212) 967-8800 or (800) 322-8755.

You can find Chelsea House on the World Wide Web at
http://www.chelseahouse.com

Text design by Lina Farinella
Cover design by Alicia Post
Composition by Newgen
Cover printed by Bang Printing, Brainerd, Minn.
Book printed and bound by Bang Printing, Brainerd, Minn.
Date printed: October 2010
Printed in the United States of America

10 9 8 7 6 5 4 3 2 1
This book is printed on acid-free paper.

All links and Web addresses were checked and verified to be correct at the time of publication. Because of the dynamic nature of the Web, some addresses and links may have changed since publication and may no longer be valid.

Contents

Foreword
by Paul C. Rosier

Native American words, phrases, and tribal names are embedded in the very geography of the United States—in the names of creeks, rivers, lakes, cities, and states, including Alabama, Connecticut, Iowa, Kansas, Illinois, Missouri, Oklahoma, and many others. Yet Native Americans remain the most misunderstood ethnic group in the United States. This is a result of limited coverage of Native American history in middle schools, high schools, and colleges; poor coverage of contemporary Native American issues in the news media; and stereotypes created by Hollywood movies, sporting events, and TV shows.

Two newspaper articles about American Indians caught my eye in recent months. Paired together, they provide us with a good introduction to the experiences of American Indians today: first, how they are stereotyped and turned into commodities; and second, how they see themselves being a part of the United States and of the wider world. (Note: I use the terms *Native Americans* and *American Indians* interchangeably; both terms are considered appropriate.)

In the first article, "Humorous Souvenirs to Some, Offensive Stereotypes to Others," written by Carol Berry in *Indian Country Today,* I read that tourist shops in Colorado were selling "souvenir" T-shirts portraying American Indians as drunks. "My Indian name is Runs with Beer," read one T-shirt offered in Denver. According to the article, the T-shirts are "the kind of stereotype-reinforcing products also seen in nearby Boulder, Estes Park, and likely other Colorado communities, whether as part of the tourism trade or as everyday merchandise." No other ethnic group in the United States is stereotyped in such a public fashion. In addition, Native people are used to sell a range of consumer goods, including the Jeep Cherokee, Red Man chewing tobacco, Land O'Lakes butter, and other items that either objectify or insult them, such as cigar store Indians. As importantly, non-Indians learn about American Indian history and culture through sports teams such as the Atlanta Braves, Cleveland Indians, Florida State Seminoles, or Washington Redskins, whose name many American Indians consider a racist insult; dictionaries define *redskin* as a "disparaging" or "offensive" term for American Indians. When fans in Atlanta do their "tomahawk chant" at Braves baseball games, they perform two inappropriate and related acts: One, they perpetuate a stereotype of American Indians as violent; and two, they tell a historical narrative that covers up the violent ways that Georgians treated the Cherokee during the Removal period of the 1830s.

The second article, written by Melissa Pinion-Whitt of the San Bernardino *Sun* addressed an important but unknown dimension of Native American societies that runs counter to the irresponsible and violent image created by products and sporting events. The article, "San Manuels Donate $1.7 M for Aid to Haiti," described a Native American community that had sent aid to Haiti after it was devastated in January 2010 by an earthquake that killed more than 200,000 people, injured hundreds of thousands more, and destroyed the Haitian capital. The San Manuel Band of Mission Indians in California donated $1.7 million to help relief efforts in Haiti; San Manuel children held fund-raisers to collect additional donations. For the San Manuel Indians it was nothing new; in 2007 they had donated $1 million to help Sudanese refugees in Darfur. San Manuel also contributed $700,000 to relief efforts following Hurricane Katrina and Hurricane Rita, and donated $1 million in 2007 for wildfire recovery in Southern California.

Such generosity is consistent with many American Indian nations' cultural practices, such as the "give-away," in which wealthy tribal members give to the needy, and the "potlatch," a winter gift-giving ceremony and feast tradition shared by tribes in the

Pacific Northwest. And it is consistent with historical accounts of American Indians' generosity. For example, in 1847 Cherokee and Choctaw, who had recently survived their forced march on a "Trail of Tears" from their homelands in the American South to present-day Oklahoma, sent aid to Irish families after reading of the potato famine, which created a similar forced migration of Irish. A Cherokee newspaper editorial, quoted in Christine Kinealy's *The Great Irish Famine: Impact, Ideology, and Rebellion,* explained that the Cherokee "will be richly repaid by the consciousness of having done a good act, by the moral effect it will produce abroad." During and after World War II, nine Pueblo communities in New Mexico offered to donate food to the hungry in Europe, after Pueblo army veterans told stories of suffering they had witnessed while serving in the United States armed forces overseas. Considering themselves a part of the wider world, Native people have reached beyond their borders, despite their own material poverty, to help create a peaceful world community.

American Indian nations have demonstrated such generosity within the United States, especially in recent years. After the terrorist attacks of September 11, 2001, the Lakota Sioux in South Dakota offered police officers and emergency medical personnel to New York City to help with relief efforts; Indian nations across the country sent millions of dollars to help the victims of the attacks. As an editorial in the *Native American Times* newspaper explained on September 12, 2001, "American Indians love this country like no other. . . . Today, we are all New Yorkers."

Indeed, Native Americans have sacrificed their lives in defending the United States from its enemies in order to maintain their right to be both American and Indian. As the volumes in this series tell us, Native Americans patriotically served as soldiers (including as "code talkers") during World War I and World War II, as well as during the Korean War, the Vietnam War, and, after 9/11, the wars in Afghanistan and Iraq. Native soldiers, men and women, do so today by the tens of thousands because they believe in America, an

America that celebrates different cultures and peoples. Sgt. Leonard Gouge, a Muscogee Creek, explained it best in an article in *Cherokee News Path* in discussing his post-9/11 army service. He said he was willing to serve his country abroad because "by supporting the American way of life, I am preserving the Indian way of life."

This new Chelsea House series has two main goals. The first is to document the rich diversity of American Indian societies and the ways their cultural practices and traditions have evolved over time. The second goal is to provide the reader with coverage of the complex relationships that have developed between non-Indians and Indians over the past several hundred years. This history helps to explain why American Indians consider themselves both American and Indian and why they see preserving this identity as a strength of the American way of life, as evidence to the rest of the world that America is a champion of cultural diversity and religious freedom. By exploring Native Americans' cultural diversity and their contributions to the making of the United States, these volumes confront the stereotypes that paint all American Indians as the same and portray them as violent; as "drunks," as those Colorado T-shirts do; or as rich casino owners, as many news accounts do.

* * *

Each of the 14 volumes in this series is written by a scholar who shares my conviction that young adult readers are both fascinated by Native American history and culture and have not been provided with sufficient material to properly understand the diverse nature of this complex history and culture. The authors themselves represent a varied group that includes university teachers and professional writers, men and women, and Native and non-Native. To tell these fascinating stories, this talented group of scholars has examined an incredible variety of sources, both the primary sources that historical actors have created and the secondary sources that historians and anthropologists have written to make sense of the past.

Although the 14 Indian nations (also called tribes and communities) selected for this series have different histories and cultures, they all share certain common experiences. In particular, they had to face an American empire that spread westward in the eighteenth and nineteenth centuries, causing great trauma and change for all Native people in the process. Because each volume documents American Indians' experiences dealing with powerful non-Indian institutions and ideas, I outline below the major periods and features of federal Indian policy-making in order to provide a frame of reference for complex processes of change with which American Indians had to contend. These periods—Assimilation, Indian New Deal, Termination, Red Power, and Self-determination—and specific acts of legislation that define them—in particular the General Allotment Act, the Indian Reorganization Act, and the Indian Self-determination and Education Assistance Act—will appear in all the volumes, especially in the latter chapters.

In 1851, the commissioner of the federal Bureau of Indian Affairs (BIA) outlined a three-part program for subduing American Indians militarily and assimilating them into the United States: concentration, domestication, and incorporation. In the first phase, the federal government waged war with the American Indian nations of the American West in order to "concentrate" them on reservations, away from expanding settlements of white Americans and immigrants. Some American Indian nations experienced terrible violence in resisting federal troops and state militia; others submitted peacefully and accepted life on a reservation. During this phase, roughly from the 1850s to the 1880s, the U.S. government signed hundreds of treaties with defeated American Indian nations. These treaties "reserved" to these American Indian nations specific territory as well as the use of natural resources. And they provided funding for the next phase of "domestication."

During the domestication phase, roughly the 1870s to the early 1900s, federal officials sought to remake American Indians in the mold of white Americans. Through the Civilization Program, which actually started with President Thomas Jefferson, federal officials sent religious missionaries, farm instructors, and teachers to the newly created reservations in an effort to "kill the Indian to save the man," to use a phrase of that time. The ultimate goal was to extinguish American Indian cultural traditions and turn American Indians into Christian yeoman farmers. The most important piece of legislation in this period was the General Allotment Act (or Dawes Act), which mandated that American Indian nations sell much of their territory to white farmers and use the proceeds to farm on what was left of their homelands. The program was a failure, for the most part, because white farmers got much of the best arable land in the process. Another important part of the domestication agenda was the federal boarding school program, which required all American Indian children to attend schools to further their rejection of Indian ways and the adoption of non-Indian ways. The goal of federal reformers, in sum, was to incorporate (or assimilate) American Indians into American society as individual citizens and not as groups with special traditions and religious practices.

During the 1930s some federal officials came to believe that American Indians deserved the right to practice their own religion and sustain their identity as Indians, arguing that such diversity made America stronger. During the Indian New Deal period of the 1930s, BIA commissioner John Collier devised the Indian Reorganization Act (IRA), which passed in 1934, to give American Indian nations more power, not less. Not all American Indians supported the IRA, but most did. They were eager to improve their reservations, which suffered from tremendous poverty that resulted in large measure from federal policies such as the General Allotment Act.

Some federal officials opposed the IRA, however, and pushed for the assimilation of American Indians in a movement called Termination. The two main goals of Termination advocates, during the 1950s and 1960s, were to end (terminate) the federal reservation system and American Indians' political sovereignty derived from treaties and to relocate American Indians from rural reservations to urban areas. These coercive federal assimilation policies in turn generated resistance from Native Americans, including young activists who helped to create the so-called Red Power era of the 1960s and 1970s, which coincided with the African-American civil rights movement. This resistance led to the federal government's rejection of Termination policies in 1970. And in 1975 the U.S. Congress passed the Indian Self-determination and Education Assistance Act, which made it the government's policy to support American Indians' right to determine the future of their communities. Congress then passed legislation to help American Indian nations to improve reservation life; these acts strengthened American Indians' religious freedom, political sovereignty, and economic opportunity.

All American Indians, especially those in the western United States, were affected in some way by the various federal policies described above. But it is important to highlight the fact that each American Indian community responded in different ways to these pressures for change, both the detribalization policies of assimilation and the retribalization policies of self-determination. There is no one group of "Indians." American Indians were and still are a very diverse group. Some embraced the assimilation programs of the federal government and rejected the old traditions; others refused to adopt non-Indian customs or did so selectively, on their own terms. Most American Indians, as I noted above, maintain a dual identity of American and Indian.

Today, there are more than 550 American Indian (and Alaska Natives) nations recognized by the federal government. They have a legal and political status similar to states, but they have special rights and privileges that are the result of congressional acts and the hundreds of treaties that still govern federal-Indian relations today. In July 2008, the total population of American Indians (and Alaska Natives) was 4.9 million, representing about 1.6 percent of the United States population. The state with the highest number of American Indians is California, followed by Oklahoma, home to the Cherokee (the largest American Indian nation in terms of population), and then Arizona, home to the Navajo (the second-largest American Indian nation). All told, roughly half of the American Indian population lives in urban areas; the other half lives on reservations and in other rural parts of the country. Like all their fellow American citizens, American Indians pay federal taxes, obey federal laws, and vote in federal, state, and local elections; they also participate in the democratic processes of their American Indian nations, electing judges, politicians, and other civic officials.

This series on the history and culture of Native Americans celebrates their diversity and differences as well as the ways they have strengthened the broader community of America. Ronnie Lupe, the chairman of the White Mountain Apache government in Arizona, once addressed questions from non-Indians as to "why Indians serve the United States with such distinction and honor?" Lupe, a Korean War veteran, answered those questions during the Gulf War of 1991–1992, in which Native American soldiers served to protect the independence of the Kuwaiti people. He explained in "Chairman's Corner" in *The Fort Apache Scout* that "our loyalty to the United States goes beyond our need to defend our home and reservation lands. . . . Only a few in this country really understand that the indigenous people are a national treasure. Our values have the potential of creating the social, environmental, and spiritual healing that could make this country truly great."

—Paul C. Rosier
Associate Professor of History
Villanova University

The Migration
of the Comanche
People

The Comanche people are believed to have originated from a Uto-Aztecan-speaking people. They call themselves Numunu, which means "the People." Others gave them a title referring to their quickness to battle; their current name, the Comanche, came from a Spanish term that roughly translates to mean "quick to fight."

When in 1492 Christopher Columbus "discovered" what was to become known as America, the rest of the world hailed his achievement with laud and honor. They viewed this with the bigotry typical of the time: with an egocentric worldview and superiority that marked this era as the beginning of tragic events in the lives of Native Americans. Europeans living then did not begin to consider that millions of human beings already lived on the continent Columbus had inadvertently stumbled upon. But this gets ahead of our tale of the Comanche, who in their heyday became known (and feared) as the Lords of the Southern Plains.

In the time known as the pre-Columbian Era, the people now called Native Americans had their own cultures, traditions, ways of life, and deities. They had a rich existence and vibrant history. The Comanche are a part of that demographic group.

Since the histories of Native American peoples as a whole were passed orally from one generation to the next, not much is known about them before they were "discovered" by the rest of the world. There are, however, many theories and explanations as to how these people arrived on the continent of North America.

THE BERING STRAIT MIGRATION

Most historians and scientists agree that the majority of Native American Indians migrated from Asia. Long ago, a slender thread of land between what is now known as Siberia and Alaska brought together the European and American continents. The prehistoric peoples traversed this "land bridge" across the Bering Sea. On a great migration, which was to last at least a thousand years, the prehistoric peoples traversed the land bridge across the Bering Strait and settled on the American continents.

The debate, however, has continued to rage over the genetic origins of the Native Americans. Did they really come from Asia? How can this be proved?

In 1991, a biochemist by the name of Douglas C. Wallace of Emory University in Atlanta, Georgia, claimed he had irrefutable proof of Native Americans' Asian origin. Wallace took blood samples from 99 different living subjects, each with a different maternal ancestry, to study their mitochondrial DNA. The samples he took were from three geographically disparate groups of Indians: the Ticuna Indians of South America, the Maya of Central America, and the Pima of North America. Wallace detected rare chemical sequences in the mitochondrial DNA of the samples and

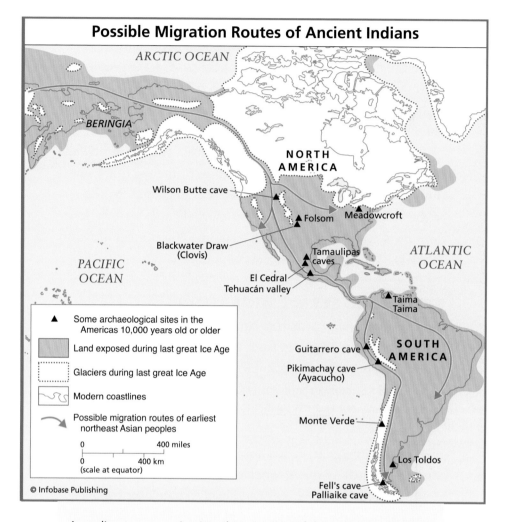

Possible Migration Routes of Ancient Indians

ARCTIC OCEAN

BERINGIA

NORTH AMERICA

Wilson Butte cave

Folsom   Meadowcroft

Blackwater Draw (Clovis)

Tamaulipas caves

El Cedral
Tehuacán valley

Taima Taima

PACIFIC OCEAN

ATLANTIC OCEAN

SOUTH AMERICA

Guitarrero cave

Pikimachay cave (Ayacucho)

Monte Verde

Los Toldos

Fell's cave
Palliaike cave

▲ Some archaeological sites in the Americas 10,000 years old or older

Land exposed during last great Ice Age

Glaciers during last great Ice Age

Modern coastlines

Possible migration routes of earliest northeast Asian peoples

0   400 miles
0   400 km
(scale at equator)

© Infobase Publishing

According to many scientists, the migration of the indigenous peoples of the Americas may have taken place some 12,000 to 50,000 years ago. Scientists speculate that humans migrated from Asia across Beringia, a former land bridge roughly 1,000 miles (1,609.3 km) long.

found that these sequences occurred only in the DNA of Asian populations. The obvious conclusion is that the Indians occupying the American continent originally came from Asia. Wallace did not find this chemical sequence in Inuit, Navajos, Aleuts, and other tribes who, he said, arrived on this continent at a later date.

Wallace further claimed to have traced the DNA lineages of these tribes to at least four women in an early migrating group. While Wallace theorizes that the Bering Strait trek first occurred 15,000 to 30,000 years ago, there are conflicting hypotheses.

Geneticist Svante Paabo of the University of California, Berkeley, argued against some of Wallace's findings. Paabo claims the tribes of the Pacific Northwest share commonalities with 30, rather than four, different mitochondrial DNA sequences; he further argues that the crossing of the Bering Strait took place 40,000 to 50,000 years ago. Whenever they arrived, however, the predecessors of the Native Americans began settling in and multiplying on the continent that is now North America.

TRIBAL ORIGINS: THE COMANCHE AND THE SHOSHONE

From the Bering Strait, the ancestors of the Native Americans traveled south; the people who would become the Comanche eventually settled in the area known as the Southern Plains region of what would become the United States. Researchers know this because the Comanche share the same linguistic heritage with other tribes in the northwestern region of what is now the United States. Historical linguists have traced dialectical similarities in tribes related to the Comanche, such as the Ute and the Shoshone, the latter of which were at one time united with the Comanche.

Anthropologists have determined that the Comanche and the Shoshone were one people until approximately 1700, when for some reason, they became two separate groups. Some oral histories indicate that the two groups became hostile toward each other. One story says it began with an argument over which group had killed a bear; another story holds that it began with a fight between a boy from each band, which resulted in one boy killing the other.

Whatever the reason for their parting, in the 1700s, the Shoshone settled in what is now Wyoming and Montana; the

Comanche people settled in parts of what would become Texas, New Mexico, Colorado, and Kansas. This region was called "The Comancheria," which means "Land of the Comanche."

THE INFLUENCE OF THE HORSE

The Comancheria was a vast area of more than 24,000 square miles (62,160 square kilometers). Before Spanish explorers came, the Comanche were obliged to hunt and travel on foot. To carry their burdens when moving camp, they depended upon their camp dogs to carry much of their possessions. The Comanche attached a contraption called a travois to the dogs' backs, enabling them to do much of the moving of the camp.

When Spanish explorers first arrived in the early 1500s, they brought with them an animal not indigenous (native) to this continent: the horse. When Native Americans, including the Comanche, obtained this animal in approximately 1680, their entire existence changed.

Authors Ernest Wallace and E. Adamson Hoebel wrote about the importance of the horse in their book, *The Comanches: Lords of the South Plains.* Wallace and Hoebel write that because of the horse, hunters could roam farther and faster in search of game and bring back more meat on the horses' backs. The tribes could move farther and more quickly with the help of their equine ally. Horses became a new kind of status symbol for hunters and warriors alike: Now, they were no longer eking out an existence on the plains—they were in charge of their own destiny. The horse became not only a status symbol, but a new form of wealth. When a warrior owned a herd of them, it was a sign of prosperity and the man's ability to provide for his wives and family and, as such, became an offering when a man was courting his bride.

The advent of the horse into the Comanche world changed every aspect of their lives. They, along with other tribes, such as the Arapaho, Ute, Cheyenne, Crow, Kiowa, and Osage, took up a nomadic lifestyle on the Great Plains with zeal. With the help of the horse and the ferocity and tenacity of the Comanche, they began to thrive; by the mid-1800s, their population swelled to 20,000 to 45,000, depending on varying accounts.

Among all the Native people living on the plains, the Comanche also became known as the best horse riders and trainers, and

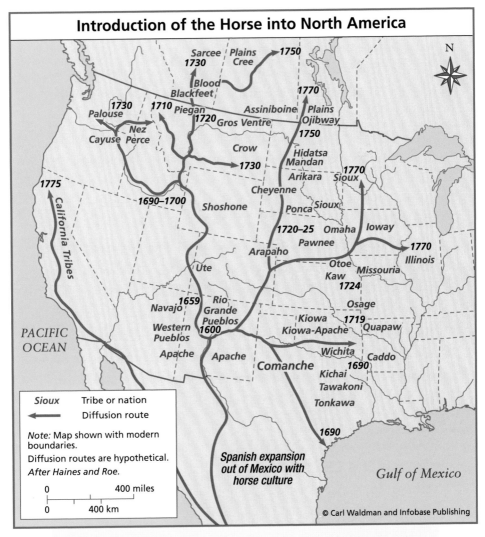

Introduction of the Horse into North America

Spanish settlers first introduced the horse to Native Americans, bringing them over from their homeland as they settled colonies along the Rio Grande in the late 1590s. Although the indigenous peoples were first frightened of the large animal, indigenous tribes soon managed to master the horse. The horse proved to be a valuable asset to Native American communities.

children at a very early age were taught to ride. Fearless warriors and hunters, the Comanche became adept at riding at a full gallop, shooting an enemy or a buffalo while hanging from under the horse's neck. Artists such as Frederick Remington and George Catlin became famous for their paintings of this era; they traveled and lived among many Native American nations, including the Comanche. Their artistic depictions of Comanche hunters and warriors in action are still famous today.

The advent of the horse allowed not only for the population of the Comanche to grow and prosper: now, they could better protect themselves against other Native American nations and settlers coming into the Comancheria. From 1720 to the 1850s, the Comanche successfully battled other Native nations, such as the Osage, Arapaho, and Pawnee, drove out the Apache from the Southern Plains, and fought the advances of Spanish and French settlers.

Author Pekka Hamalainen has stated that the Comanche were much more than fighters against such advances. In his book *The Comanche Empire*, he states that they were launched in what he called "an explosive expansion" against what was then "the world's largest empire"—Spain. He goes on further to state that the Comanche refused to become passive victims during the expansionist era. This staunch, unrelenting attitude would help them survive the difficult times to come.

TRAINING A WILD HORSE: "ONE WITH THE WIND"

Perhaps no Native American nation has had a more spiritual relationship with the horse than the Comanche. Early on, they recognized that horses were pack animals and would follow a leader—but not an abusive one. The Comanche watched the horses as they behaved in herds and individually and learned from these observations ways in which they might train them.

An adept horse trainer could have a horse under his command in as little as a few hours. While white trainers sought to subdue and "break" the horse with whip and spur, the Comanche horse trainer's goal was to become one with the horse and lead the horse to understand that the trainer was the herd "leader," in part by using gestures and whispers. The successful horse trainer prepared a horse to follow, turn, walk backward, and even lie down, all in quick order, and all in nearly total silence. Nick Mejia, great-grandson of Comanche chief Quanah Parker, explained, "The horse was seen as more than an animal—he was your partner. He was a brother."

It was important to train a horse through these "quiet" methods for a number of reasons. First, the Comanche knew this was the most effective method; second, when on the hunt or when evading or preparing to attack the enemy, silence was important for a successful outcome.

The Comanche not only were the best horse trainers, but they became excellent horse breeders as well, castrating the male horses that carried undesirable traits and breeding those with traits they wanted, such as disposition and even temperament. In Hamalainen's book, he wrote of one U.S. Army officer, Theodore Ayrault Dodge, who visited the Comancheria in the 1850s. "In one particular," Hamalainen quoted as Dodge recorded in a journal, "the Comanche is noteworthy. He knows more about a horse and horse-breeding than any other Indian." He added, "The corollary to this is that the Comanche is far less cruel to his beasts, and though he begins to use them as yearlings, the ponies often last through many years."

A Native American named GaWaNi Pony Boy is the author of several books on horse training. In his book, *Out of the Saddle*, he writes: "There is only one thing that stands between horse and rider performing as one creature; only one hurdle that separates the perfect combination of two- and four-legged; only one stumbling block that awaits the horse and rider who wish to act as one.

The Comanche peoples were thought to be the greatest horsemen in the world. Due to the tribe's riding and training skills and their proficiency in breeding, capturing, and trading horses, the Comanche herds massively outnumbered those of other tribes. In fact, the Comanche language became the standard of horse trading on the plains.

It is communication. A horse and rider who can communicate successfully can do anything—*anything*!" Pony Boy states further that, with the trainer as the "herd leader," the horse would learn from and eventually follow him or her. He also stresses the importance of praise to the horse: "If the horse has performed well," he writes, "let him know it. Tell him you are grateful for his companionship. For centuries, Native Americans were taught this natural politeness. They brought that teaching into their relationship with the animal and found it to be beneficial in establishing the needed closeness and respect that made them, and their horse, one with the wind."

THE COMANCHE AND THE FRENCH

The acquisition of the horse led to greater competition for the Comanche to acquire modern-day tools. Thus, in the 1720s, they realized they could have an advantage if they befriended French traders. These traders gave the Comanche much-needed tools, such as guns and other weapons, metal tools, and ammunition, in exchange for the horses and mules the Comanche obtained in their raiding forays against Spanish settlers. These raids increased along with the desire for more and better goods from the French traders; over time, the raids extended not only into Spanish settlements but included Pueblo Indian settlements in Texas and Mexico. The Spanish government became increasingly concerned about the threat the Comanche posed to their settlers—and their territorial claims. Something would have to be done.

Part of the solution to this dilemma came about when Louisiana was ceded to Spain. Before 1763, the French colony of Louisiana included the present-day states of Louisiana, Mississippi, Arkansas, Oklahoma, Missouri, Kansas, Nebraska, Iowa, Illinois, Indiana, Michigan, Wisconsin, Minnesota, North Dakota, and South Dakota. This area and the settlement of Natchitoches (in present-day northwest Louisiana) established trade between the Spanish and the French. After the French and Indian War (1754–1763), fought between Great Britain and France over control of New France (a French colony in Canada), France ceded Canada to Great Britain and transferred Louisiana to Spain, and Spain ceded Florida to Great Britain. Now Spain could control how the Comanche people dealt with the French traders, and raids would eventually cease. By 1786, the raids, carried on to trade with the French, were almost negligible.

MAKING PEACE: THE KIOWA AND THE SPANISH

Before 1790, the Kiowa, too, were a people against whom the Comanche fought. By roughly 1790, however, this situation changed, and, with the help of Spain, the two nations made peace. It was in summer of that year that the two groups set up an encampment together, hunting buffalo and sharing a sun dance (although the Comanche did not usually practice this, the Kiowa did). The Kiowa today are still a valuable ally to modern-day Comanche.

The sun dance was a religious ceremony common to the Native American tribes of the Great Plains. Although each tribe had its own distinct rituals, many had features in common. Young men of the tribes would gather in a circle and sing, dance, fast, experience visions, pray, and sometimes pierce the skin on their chest, arms, and back as a religious offering to the Great Mystery, or Creator.

The Spanish had made peace earlier with the Comanche when they sent troops into Comanche territory in the summer of 1779. Led by Don Juan Bautista de Anza, the troops were joined by Ute and Apache warriors, who attacked some Comanche. Their tribal war chief, Green Horn, was killed in that attack. This led to peace talks between the Comanche and the Spanish. With a Comanche leader named Leather Jacket making negotiations with the Spanish on behalf of his people, the Spanish agreed to reestablish trade with the Comanche if they would cease making raids against Spanish settlers. Ironically enough, part of this agreement allied the Comanche with the Spanish—against the Pawnee and the Apache, the latter tribe of which had helped the Spanish in the "peacemaking" attack.

This truce between Spain and the Comanche lasted for approximately 50 years and would probably have lasted longer except for the divisions among the Comanche themselves. Across the Comancheria, bands of Comanche were scattered like clouds across a midwestern summer sky, and each band had its own traditions and way of life. At that time, there were six divisions of Comanche.

In the central part of the Comancheria were three of these divisions, or bands. One was called the Tanimas, which means "Liver Eaters"; another was called the Tenawas, meaning "Those

Who Stay Downstream"; and the third was called the Nokonis, which means "Those Who Turn Back." Far to the south were the Penatekas, or "Honey Eaters." To the north were the last two divisions: the Kotsotekas, or "Buffalo Eaters," and the Yamparika, or "Root Eaters." Due to distance, there was little interband unity, and the bands in the south did not believe that the truce with the Spanish applied to them. They persisted in going on raiding forays against the Spanish settlers in Texas, taking horses and cattle and trading their loot for guns and other supplies in New Mexico.

For some 150 years, the Comanche were the Lords of the Southern Plains, raiding, taking captives for slaves or to trade, capturing horses, and inspiring fear in the hearts of settlers and enemy nations. As they dominated the Southern Plains, little did the Comanche know that the times to come would challenge them in every way and not only endanger their way of life but their very existence as a people.

Culture, Religion, and Traditions

It remains a sensitive point for most Native Americans when others say America was discovered by Christopher Columbus. Not only do history scholars and archaeologists say now that other explorers were here before him (such as the Vikings, who are even said to have traded with Native people), but before his arrival, the continent was already teeming with a great variety of people. These people had their own social systems, diplomatic protocols, traditions, and ways of life. They have been preserved through generations of people passing on their history through stories told to the young.

Like other Native Americans, the Comanche have a tradition of passing their history orally. Each generation tells the stories of Earth's beginnings, as well as stories of heroes and villains, to the next generation.

The Earth, and everything in, on, and surrounding it, was a source of great mystery and wonder to Native Americans; the environment into which the Comanche settled was enough to humble and awe anyone. The Comancheria was ruled by quick-silver weather conditions, from raging prairie storms or bone-cracking cold winds to still, hot days that might only be relieved by pounding hailstorms and heart-stopping flash floods. The great expanse of endless prairie lands teeming with all types of wild animals must have made the Comanche of old feel more than a little overwhelmed.

Especially in the days when there were no scientific explanations for natural phenomena, stories were created to explain them. These explanations became legends and helped the Comanche live in harmony with the world around them. What follows are a few of the stories that have survived many winters of telling and retelling.

THE LEGEND OF MANITOU SPRINGS

Before the white man came to the land of the Comanche, and when they were one with the Shoshone, there were two hunters out on a foray in the Rocky Mountains. One had enjoyed great luck in the hunt and had a fat deer upon his back. The other had no luck in the hunt. Both, however, were tired and thirsty.

They came upon a spring, and both fell upon it to drink. First, though, the hunter who had had the good luck in hunting took a handful of spring water and offered it to the Great Spirit Manitou, in thanks for the meat he would be bringing his family. The other hunter did not give an offering but drank his fill of the sweet spring water.

When he saw the lucky hunter give the water offering, the unlucky hunter was filled with a jealous rage, and he picked a fight. He drowned the lucky hunter in the spring.

As the unlucky hunter looked down on the drowned man, the murderer was filled with regret, but it was too late. Just then, a figure appeared to the unlucky hunter: It was an aged American Indian holding a war club. He struck down the unlucky hunter, and when the hunter fell dead into the spring, it made the water rank and undrinkable. The aged American Indian then struck a rock, and from this flowed sweet, clear water.

It is said that the two hunters represent the Shoshone and Comanche nations, and this is one story behind their separation. That is one Comanche legend of how Manitou Springs came to be.

THE VISION QUEST AND PERSONAL MEDICINE

In traditional Native American culture, the word *medicine* is not something that one takes for an ache or pain. *Merriam Webster's Collegiate Dictionary* defines this particular form of the word to mean "an object held in traditional American Indian belief to give control over natural or magical forces," but it means a bit more than merely that.

To Native Americans, medicine means something that gives a person special protection, talents, or gifts. For a Comanche boy, the quest for his personal medicine was a part of growing up. The "vision quest" included fasting alone for several days in the wilderness. If the boy was lucky, this part of coming into manhood resulted in a vision, often of an animal. This vision would reveal to the young man his special gifts, talents, or strengths. The animal in the vision would become the young man's symbol of protection. The experience of the vision would help the young man determine the path of his future. Visions and medicine were not merely relegated to young males. Young females, too, aspired to gain their own vision, and even the older and wiser people of the tribe paid close attention to what they might learn in their visions.

HOW THE BUFFALO CAME TO THE COMANCHE PEOPLE

In the early days of humankind, an omniscient being owned the buffalo. The being was known as "Humpback." Humpback lived with his son in a place distant from the Comanche and would not share the buffalo with them, so they could not use the buffalo's hide for shelter, its bones for tools, or its meat for food.

An animal known among the Comanche for its mischievous nature was the coyote. In those days, Coyote was able to speak. Coyote called the Comanche to a council meeting and told them to go camp near where Humpback lived and see how the buffalo were kept. They did and to their dismay saw that Humpback kept the buffalo enclosed in a corral with high stone walls—and there was only one way into the corral, through the back door of Humpback's house.

They told this to Coyote, who came up with a plan to get the buffalo to release themselves. Coyote changed himself into a bird called a killdeer and waited for Humpback's son to come to a nearby spring for water. When the boy did, Coyote pretended to have a broken wing, and the boy picked him up. The boy wanted to keep the bird for a pet, but his father would not let him, and he made him release the bird. Coyote then changed himself into a dog, and when the boy found him near the spring the next day, Humpback allowed his son to keep the dog as a pet, but he would have to keep his new pet in the pen with the buffalo. This, of course, was exactly what Coyote wanted.

That night, after Humpback and his son were asleep, Coyote ran among the buffalo, barking loudly and nipping at their heels. The buffalo stampeded and broke down the stone walls of their pen. Ever since then, the buffalo have been among the Comanche.

This story has been recounted in many different versions, including Wallace and Hoebel's book, *The Comanches: Lords of the South Plains*. Perhaps the earliest published version of this story was in the July-September 1909 issue of *Journal of American Folklore*.

THE BUFFALO AND COMANCHE SPIRITUALITY

Traditionally, the buffalo was the most revered of all the animals on the Southern Plains, and the quest for the animal took on near-zealous proportions. When one considers all the uses with which the buffalo provided the Comanche—giving them the basics of food, clothing, and shelter—it is easy to understand this reverence toward the bison.

First, of course, buffalo was desired for its meat. The liver and tongue were the most valued (and the latter came to be considered

The buffalo was considered sacred to the Plains Indians. This animal was the largest source of items and not a single part went unused. Pictured is a buffalo hide robe bearing the Sacred Circle, which is a symbol of harmony and attests to the maturity of the robe's wearer.

a delicacy among Europeans). Cuts that were of lesser quality were cut into strips, pounded with berries, then dried; they became a kind of jerky called pemmican, which was consumed when on the hunt or otherwise on the move.

Bones were made into tools; the shoulder bone might become a shovel; smaller bones were made into sewing awls or gaming pieces. The hide of the buffalo was stretched, scraped, and tanned and became tipi coverings, moccasins, or clothing; the fur might be used for cold-weather clothing, headdresses, or other decoration. Some organs, such as the stomach, might become a vessel with which to hold water. The resilient, sinewy ligaments were often made into bowstring or sewing thread. Horns and fur were used for the making of headdresses, and hooves were used as rattles for ceremonial times. Even the skull, when cleaned and dried, was used in religious ceremonies. Virtually nothing was thrown away.

William Hornaday, who lived from 1854 to 1937, rose to prominence in the world of conservation, and in 1882, he was made chief taxidermist of the U.S. National Museum at the Smithsonian Institution. In 1886, when he traveled to the Great Plains to research the existing bison herds, he was shocked and saddened at how the great herds had dwindled. Smithsonian Institution archives describe how, in Hornaday's report on the "extermination" of the buffalo on the plains, he said that at the height of their population, the bison numbered as many as 100 million head. One herd alone, seen in 1871, was said to have numbered approximately 4 million. Other accounts, such as those of the early American explorers Meriwether Lewis and William Clark, described seeing a herd begin crossing a river by morning, and by sunset that same herd would still be crossing. It is difficult to imagine now that herds of such magnitude once freely roamed the Great Plains.

In 1889, when Hornaday published *The Extermination of the American Bison*, his work helped keep the bison from certain and complete extinction. He ultimately became the founder of the American conservationist movement.

RELIGION IN EVERYDAY LIFE

Religion, or a sense of spirituality, was a part of every waking moment in the life of a Comanche. Even today, the Comanche give reverence toward such everyday, ordinary acts as waking, speaking, sharing a meal, or working, all of which are preceded by prayer or songs of praise. An example of daily spirituality was in the old days of visiting another person's tipi. Upon coming to another's tipi, the visitor would walk around the tipi once, then stand waiting at the tipi door flap. This walk-around honored the lodge and those dwelling within and allowed time for those inside to be aware of and make ready for their guest(s), whom they then invited inside.

In his book *Mystic Warriors of the Plains*, author Thomas E. Mails discusses how different Native etiquette is from non-Indian manners. He writes that it was customary also (and is to this day among the Comanche) that when one visited, the purpose for the visit was not discussed immediately. It was considered good manners to allow the visitor(s) to make themselves comfortable, have some food and perhaps share a pipe, and to wait upon the talk (this was one custom that has historically seemed to make European visitors a bit nervous, for they were accustomed to telling their business right away, and silence was regarded as unnatural).

In the taking of food, prayer was always offered first and a bit of the food held toward the four cardinal directions in thanks. In the making of weapons, such as arrows, there were certain songs sung and the making of them was surrounded by ritual. Even in such simple everyday practices as the taking of a morning bath, there were songs sung in thanksgiving for the new day. To the Comanche, it is believed that all aspects of life are sacred, as life itself is a gift from God.

Weapons and Tools Used by the Comanche

Not only were the Comanche the best horsemen, but they used the bow and arrow with deadly precision. Part of the reason for this is due to their reputation as the best arrow makers of the Southern Plains. Comanche hunters used woods such as dogwood, ash, or mulberry for the body of the arrow itself, and for fletching, they chose feathers from the buzzard, turkey, or owl.

Comanche men were the ones who made their weapons and tools, and most of these were made by the elder men in the tribe when they had outgrown their ability to go on the hunt or on the warpath. As in all aspects of daily life, even the making of weapons was conducted with a certain spirituality in the way of singing songs, as the makers asked for protection for the weapons' owners in the hunt or in battle.

ALLIES AND ENEMIES: THE APACHE

Before reservation life, the Apache were constantly at war with the Comanche. The clan of Apache known as the Lipan allied quickly with the Spanish against the Comanche. The Lipan also accepted Spain's response on the incursion, or raids, of Spanish missions— which were, often as not, destroyed by the Comanche. The Apache were at the height of their power until the late 1700s, when the Comanche made their way into the land known as the Staked Plains. But the Lipan continued to fight the Comanche at every opportunity.

The Apache themselves were friendly with the first whites who appeared in their country, but this friendship was not to last long. In 1861, for example, U.S. soldiers met with some Apache who were working with whites, trying to make a pass through the Chiricahua Mountains. As a sign of peace, the soldiers flew a white truce flag; but instead of following through with this peaceful overture, they arrested the Apache. A fight broke out when they, understandably, resisted.

The Apache continued to fight to preserve their freedoms and way of life. They could, however, be persuaded to serve the U.S. government as scouts, and they did. General George Crook, for example, used Apache scouts to track down other Native Americans who were wanted by the government, such as the famous Apache leader Geronimo. The government also used Apache scouts to hunt down and track the Comanche people.

According to Bill Yenne's book, *The Encyclopedia of North American Indian Tribes*, the Apache were chosen as scouts for a

Before reservation life, the Comanche and the Apache peoples were often at war with each other. The Apache would ally with the Spanish against the Comanche and, later, serve the U. S. government as scouts to track down members of neighboring tribes. Pictured are Apache scouts employed by the U.S. government in 1890.

particular reason. They were known for their incredible stamina and were said to be able to travel on foot for 40 or more miles (64 km) a day; if they were on horseback, they would run the creature into the ground, stealing another when it collapsed. Like the Comanche warriors, Apache men were raised with an emphasis on endurance. They had to be able to go for long periods of time without food, water, or sleep, and if necessary to endure pain stoically. Apache tactics in raiding and attacking were successful by use of the element of surprise; they would stealthily ambush an enemy, then slip away like a dust devil on the plains. They were adroit at the art of escape, as the members of the raiding or attacking party would split up, ride far, then regroup at a place that had been previously arranged. Because of their unusual footwear—with toes upturned—the Comanche had a special name for the Apache—Ta-ashi, meaning "Turned-up." Footwear made it easier for the Comanche to track Apache warriors and raiders.

The enmity between the two nations has continued for hundreds of years. Even today, since the Apache live virtually side by side on reservation lands with the Comanche and Kiowa, there remains a kind of uneasy truce between them.

EARLY COMMERCE

Between the 1700s and the 1800s, the Comanche and other Native nations did well in their dealings with traders, especially the Spanish. The Comanche tribes had been a part of the trade fair in Taos, New Mexico, as early as 1749. Among the Comanche bands, some fared better than others in their dealings with white traders and settlers. Although the band known as the Kwahadi did not deal much with any whites until the mid-1800s, other bands did so, with varying degrees of success.

The bands known as the Yamparikas and Kotsotekas in the west became quite prosperous, but others were not so lucky. To the south, the Nokoni and the Penatekas had good early trade relations with traders, but unscrupulous whites tricked these Comanche repeatedly. By the early 1800s, they retreated from such dealings with whites and developed an attitude of insolence against traders and settlers alike. Often, Comanche warriors would raid Spanish settlements, taking horses and hostages, and then trade them in Taos, selling them back to their rightful owners. Understandably, this practice only served to create friction between the Spanish and the Comanche.

Being separated by hundreds of miles as they were, the Comanche bands had little opportunity to act as one nation in their dealings with whites. One Comanche who tried to lead the Comanche people as one united group was a man named Ecuera-capa, or "Leather Jacket." His position as "head chief" was encouraged by a Spaniard by the name of Don Juan Bautista de Anza, a frontiersman in what is now New Mexico. It was said that Ecuera-capa represented the interests of more than 600 Comanche families living in the western part of the Staked Plains and through his influence helped bring about a kind of begrudging peace between Spanish settlers and western Comanche. This peace began in 1786 and held for many years. A further result of this peace was that the Comanche's raiding of Spanish settlements was put to an end.

According to Thomas E. Mails's book *Dog Soldiers, Bear Men and Buffalo Women*, unlike many other plains nations that had warrior societies, Comanche men did not usually hold to this practice. Their groups were not usually very formal and also were temporary. They did, however, have war leaders. These war chiefs wore feathered warbonnets (although a lower order wore a bonnet of a buffalo scalp).

The warbonnet wearer received this gift through friends who thought him worthy of the honor. The wearer was expected to be a leader in battle and to make his friends proud; failure to do so would lead to ridicule.

Mails points out further that a Comanche war leader could only retreat in battle after all the other warriors were safe, and the warbonnet must be protected from destruction at all costs. Failure to do this would lead to disgrace in the tribe. If, in battle, the war leader lost the warbonnet, anyone else could pick it up and become the new war leader.

MEN'S ORGANIZATIONS

Although, according to Mails, Comanche men did not actually establish societies as other tribes did, they had more loosely organized groups. In addition to those who wore the warbonnet, there were semimilitary or dance groups. Some of these went by such names as the Shield, the Little Pony, the Gourd, or the Buffalo. Competition for new members was fierce among these groups, and each group had its own songs, dances, and regalia (special clothing or accessories). Members of the groups shared in a type of brotherhood and went to war and on raids together.

Yet another type of person, was a man who became known as a "Crazy." As the name implies, a Crazy was not expected to make sense or even act in a logical way. If he did something bizarre, such as talk backward, or if he played music in the middle of the night, it was almost expected and no one paid much attention to it. In battle, he might also stake himself to the ground via a sash, and he would stay there until the battle was over or he was killed. A Crazy was a rare thing among the Comanche people, but such a person was considered to be quite brave.

Besides roles held by men in Comanche society, there were other roles that were just as important that were carried out by Comanche women.

Women in Comanche Culture

Historically, non-Indians portrayed Native American women as not much higher in stature than the camp dogs. They were written about as those who performed the thankless jobs of carrying out the drudgery of the camp—caring for the children, cooking the meals, tending to their homes, setting up and taking down their camp—and until recently, little more than this has been written about them.

Traditionally, too, artists have portrayed Native American women as either regal, innocent children of nature, or savage, immoral heathens. As early as the 1600s, artists such as Adrien Collaert II depicted Native American women as so-called Indian queens: bare breasted, crowned with feathers, and wearing a skirt of plant leaves. This artist, as well as others of his time, showed Native women in tune with their natural world, even as they dominated it.

Fast-forward 200 years, and this image has changed. Beginning around the 1700s, Native women were shown as thinner, less dominant and regal in appearance, and lighter skinned. As time went by, they began to be portrayed as more like Greek goddesses than as Native American women.

TRADITIONAL WAY OF LIFE (PRE-RESERVATION)

It is a tragic thing that, while many Native American men have become iconic legends in history, most of the women have fallen through the proverbial cracks of history. It is up to the historians of today to show that women were so much more than those who performed the duties of domestic drudgery. Rather, they were healers, warriors, artists, and farmers. They were the shapers of generations.

Similarly, female deities were positive ones, and they reflected the reverence tribes had for women. In general, men recognized the important contributions made by women in the tribe, and women were honored and even revered for those contributions.

One major difference between Native American families and white society is that, while white society considered generational progression through the males, Native Americans, including the Comanche, traced their lineage through the females. This is called a matrilineal society. The matrilineal ancestry was traced through a female figure called a "clan mother." This lineage of tracing one's roots through the women in the family, rather than the men, tells of the important role women held among the Comanche.

Women born into any clan of the Comanche were raised with more freedom of choice than European women of the same era. Comanche girls were expected to learn at their grandmothers' and mothers' sides the art of keeping a home, raising children, and domestic duties such as butchering animals and preparing food. If they showed an interest in something besides these things, they were encouraged to learn more about it. Many shamans, for example, were women.

In relationships between young, single men and women, it was usually the Comanche maiden who approached the male of her choice, rather than the other way around. If a boy approached a girl this was considered not only unacceptable but an extreme breach of tribal etiquette.

The women born into a Comanche clan had traditional roles similar to other Plains Indians. They were in charge of cooking, cleaning, gathering fruits and berries, setting up camp, transporting household goods, and caring for the children. Pictured is a George Catlin painting of an American Indian woman.

Couples were not allowed to be seen in public, so they would meet secretly, under cover of darkness. Sometimes a more forward and daring girl would creep into her lover's tipi at night. Although premarital sex was not encouraged, it was not totally frowned upon, Nonetheless, unmarried girls wanted to keep their reputations untarnished.

Comanche women might practice medicine alongside their husbands. People who were sick might come to the wife first, before asking for help from her husband. According to Carolyn Niethammer, who wrote *Daughters of the Earth: The Lives and Legends of American Indian Women*, "the only way a woman in that tribe could acquire healing power was through her husband." She also states that the woman could become a healer after the death of her husband and if the woman was also postmenopausal (this statement is said not always to be the case, however, according to interviews with some tribal elders such as LaDonna Harris).

Menstruation was viewed by the Comanche people as something quite powerful, and a woman who was "in her moon," as they called it, was forbidden to attend ceremonies for fear that the woman's power would eclipse the power of the ceremony and/or the shaman (this is still practiced today). In the past, Comanche people thought that menstrual blood nullified a man's power in his tipi, so every menses, the wife left her husband's tipi, going to her own or to her parents' tipi. After menstruation, she would purify herself with a sweat bath and return to her husband's tipi.

Young Comanche girls were not only taught how to do all the things that would be required of them when they became a wife and mother, but as they toiled beside their female relatives, much of the tribe's oral history and traditions were passed on to them as well. They were taught all about etiquette expected of them as part of the tribe, what their social obligations were, and tribal customs. Comanche girls were often raised by women other than their mothers; they also called their aunts "Mother" and often were closer to their grandmothers than to their mothers. According to

Comanche LaDonna Harris, who teaches classes on the Comanche in Albuquerque, New Mexico, "The children, not just the girls, were raised by the tribe. Everyone saw it as his or her duty to help in the rearing of the children."

One major lesson taught to young girls regarded the butchering and preparing of buffalo. Their lesson began at the time of the kill, right after the buffalo hunt. First the women skinned the bison; this had to be done before the animal's body cooled, as skinning a newly dead animal was much easier than skinning one that had been killed several hours previously.

The tools for skinning and preparing the bison were simple and few. The main tool was a scraper, which was flat and made of stone. It was smooth, so a woman could use her hands to scrape the hide from the flesh without tearing her own skin. Tools made of bone were also used to abrade the hide to make it easier to tan. A large, broad bone, such as a shoulder blade from another buffalo, was used to make robes soft.

Once the woman skinned the buffalo, the hide was laid on the ground and attached there by stakes (also sometimes it was hung upright on a frame). The woman would scrape the hide that was secured in this manner, removing hair if that was desired. When the hide was of uniform thinness, she would rub a fatty mixture of brains and liver into the skin to make it soft.

Hides had different uses: Hides with the fur left on would be made into robes and bedding; hides that had been scraped smooth were cut into shapes to fit a tipi. It might take anywhere from a dozen to more than 20 such hides to make a tipi, depending on the size of the tipi frame.

Women did not work alone but helped each other in these chores. Working together for the common good was in the Comanche woman's lifeblood, and she expected it of herself as much as she expected it of others. The more efficient Comanche woman could butcher three buffalo a day. Bison expert and early American conservationist William Hornaday had estimated that one female buffalo (a cow) of average size could yield approximately

55 pounds (25 kilograms) of pemmican (dried meat pounded with berries, useful for food when on the move), and that various bones and organs were valued for other uses.

Tipis were made with great attention to efficiency: An experienced Comanche woman could strike (take down) a tipi in less than a half hour. After moving to a new location, she had her tipi reerected and ready to refurbish in about the same amount of time.

Before being forced to take up reservation life and its radically different lifestyle, many children—boys and girls—were sometimes taken from their Native tribes by raiders. The Comanche warriors were adept at sneaking up on an enemy camp or a settlers' outpost and quietly spiriting away horses, women, and children. Sometimes these captives were traded back to the original tribe in exchange for goods such as weapons or horses; other times, though, the captives embraced the new life of the camp and became one of the Comanche. An example of this is Cynthia Ann Parker.

By the middle of the nineteenth century, Native American girls in the midwestern states were still generally taught at home, as opposed to those being raised in the East (Mount Holyoke and Oberlin colleges were open to Native American students).

By the end of that century, however, assimilation was the educational philosophy, and Native American girls were forced to attend schools, often run by the government or missionaries. There, they were punished for speaking their Comanche tongue, practicing their customs, following their own tribal religion, or even wearing their hair in the traditional braids.

WOMEN: BIRTH TO OLD AGE

All babies, male or female, were regarded as gifts from the Great Mystery. When it came time for a baby to come into the world, he or she was born in a makeshift lodge away from the rest of the camp. If the woman's labor began while the band was on the move, she stopped, gave birth with the aid of another woman or two, and rejoined the group as soon as she could. While male babies were

Cynthia Ann Parker

One of the most famous stories of captivity by Native Americans is the true story of Cynthia Ann Parker. She was one of the original white settlers in Texas, living in Fort Parker, Texas, in 1836. At that time, she was only nine years old, and the number of white settlers in the fort was about 30 altogether.

Up until that time, Cynthia Ann Parker lived like any other child of white settlers; but one day in early May of that year, her life changed. Some Comanche raiders came upon the fort and asked the guard at the gate for food. When he refused, the raiders killed him, then set about killing all the men inside the fort.

They killed many other people, too, and took livestock, food, and some of the white settlers with them. Some of these people they ransomed back to other whites, in exchange for food and horses, but a few of the children remained with the tribe. Two of these were Cynthia Ann and her brother, John, who was only six years old at the time.

The brother and sister took to life with the Comanche readily. John liked to hunt and fish with the men, and Cynthia Ann seemed to love the free life of a young Comanche woman. Sometimes roaming white settlers or trappers would see her

usually given the name of a male relative, the mother was the person who chose a baby girl's name.

Babies were kept in a cradle board until they were old enough to walk. A cradle board was made to wear like a modern-day backpack but with extra support behind the baby's head. This backboard was also taller than the baby's head, and for a reason: If the baby was thrown off the woman's back, perhaps while she was astride a horse, the board would protect the baby's head from injury.

and offer ransom for her freedom, but she always refused. Around 1845, whites were able to persuade John to return with them to the world of his birth, and he did. Cynthia Ann, however, loved the free life of the Comanche people too much. She also loved one of the warriors.

Shortly after her brother had returned to live with some of their white relations, Cynthia Ann married the chief's son, Peta Nokona. They had three children: two sons, Quanah (which means "fragrant" in Comanche) and Pecos (which means "peanut"), and a daughter, Topsannah (meaning "Prairie Flower").

Soon after Prairie Flower's birth, white soldiers raided Cynthia Ann's encampment at a place called Palo Duro Canyon. Peta Nokona was wounded in the conflict, and Cynthia Ann and Prairie Flower were captured by the whites, who thought they were rescuing her. They took her and her baby back to live with some of her white relations.

Cynthia Ann's last days were those of grief: She learned that her husband had died of his wounds, and Prairie Flower had also died from a strange fever. Finally, Cynthia Ann herself died—some say of heartbreak.

Quanah grew up and became the last chief of the Comanche (they are now led by chairmen). Cynthia Ann and her daughter are buried at Fort Sill, and Quanah's body now rests beside them.

Swaddled and in the cradle board, the baby could be carried around on the mother's back or leaned in this manner against a tree, so the baby could watch its mother as she worked, tanning hides or gathering berries. Sometimes, a baby who cried simply for attention was hung by its cradle board in a tree limb and left there for a short time. Eventually, the baby would learn that crying unnecessarily would result in this isolation and would abstain from this potentially dangerous habit. (The

For the first year of life, infants were carried in cradle boards and kept close to their mother. Cradle boards were safe and secure and could be leaned against a tree or tied to a saddle for traveling. Pictured is a Comanche baby in 1911.

danger lay in the noise: Early on, children had to learn the value of silence, to elude and survive the potential onslaught of enemies or predators).

Girls and boys were allowed to play together until they reached puberty, when boys began to learn the ways of hunters and warriors. Girls learned through their mothers, maternal grandmothers, and other females the skills they would need to help their future family thrive. By the age of puberty, a Comanche girl could identify and collect edible seeds and nuts, butcher a buffalo, carry water, gather firewood, make clothing and tipi covers, tan hides, cook meals, and put up and take down a tipi. With these skills and talents, by the time the girl experienced her first "moon," or period, she was considered marriageable. If she was also talented at such a fine skill as beadwork, she was considered a bride of special value.

Although sometimes marriages were arranged, most young Comanche women chose their husbands themselves. After the advent of the horse, a Comanche man would send one or more as a gift to the young woman's lodge. These horses were usually delivered by a relative, such as an uncle. If the girl accepted them into her father's herd, she also accepted the proposal; if the horses were later returned to the man's herd, she declined it.

It is important to note here that sometimes Anglo-Americans (whites) who witnessed such "proposals" mistakenly thought the prospective groom was "paying" for a bride. In truth, this gift of one or more horses was proof to the young woman's family that the young man was capable of providing for her.

As the woman grew into old age, she depended upon others to do what she could not do for herself. A talented and resourceful elderly woman would make beadwork, moccasins, or some other item in exchange for food or even shelter. As previously mentioned, it was after the woman was postmenopausal that she could become a shaman (a kind of priestess or spiritual leader).

WOMEN AS HEALERS AND SPIRITUAL LEADERS: SANAPIA, COMANCHE MEDICINE WOMAN

If a woman indicated an interest in becoming a healer or a shaman, she was trained in these ways, but not until she was postmenopausal did the candidate take an active role. According to author David E. Jones in *Sanapia: Comanche Medicine Woman*, one of the most well-known Comanche women who became a healer was Sanapia. She was born Mary Poafpybitty in 1895 near Fort Sill, Oklahoma. Her father was Comanche, her mother Comanche-Arapaho. Sanapia was the sixth of eleven children.

Sanapia's mother and her mother's brother, her maternal uncle, were both shamans (sometimes called "eagle doctors," as it was believed that the eagle was their source of healing power), and the uncle also embraced the peyote religion. Although her father turned from the "Red Road" when he converted to Christianity, Sanapia's maternal grandmother made sure the child learned all the old ways and the oral history of the Comanche.

Although Sanapia went to the reservation school, Cache Creek Mission School, in southern Oklahoma, she spent her summers learning about the herbs, songs, and other practices that could bring about healing. She was married three times and had two children and, in her own words, confessed that she lived a life she referred to as "roughing it out" before she became of age to be a shaman.

Any shaman or healer was expected to be a role model for the Comanche, and Sanapia began following this path. She used peyote in her healing practices, believing it to be a gift from God to The People.

Sanapia died, or as the Comanche say, "walked the spirit road" in 1979. In one of her last interviews, she expressed the worry that too few Comanche people were following the path of healing and spiritual seeking.

Famous Comanche Leaders in History

Born circa 1790 in Edwards Plateau, Texas, his Comanche name was Mo'pe-choko-pa, which literally translates to "Old Owl." He was civil chief of the Penateka Band, which included other famous Comanche such as Buffalo Hump and Santa Anna. He led his band in resisting Anglo settlers coming into Texas but was among the first to realize the futility of fighting the inevitable.

Perhaps the most amusing story known about Old Owl is an anecdote that occurred in 1845. Old Owl had a meeting with a Republic of Texas Indian agent named Robert Neighbors. Old Owl had brought with him more than 40 of his best warriors and demanded Neighbors feed all the men as well as care for their horses. Neighbors told Old Owl he hoped to "civilize" him and his people, after which Old Owl complimented Neighbors on his blue uniform coat. Neighbors immediately offered it to Old Owl as a gift. Directly on the heels of this, Old Owl's warriors began complimenting Neighbors on other items of his clothing and gear. Before long, he was left almost naked.

Old Owl liked Neighbors as a result, saying he was the only white man he had ever liked. He also told Neighbors something to this effect: "Instead of you making me into a fine civilized man, I'm going to turn you into a great Comanche warrior and horse thief." Neighbors did accompany Old Owl and his warriors on a raid into Mexico, the only official of the Republic of Texas ever to do so. Old Owl died in 1849, probably due to the smallpox outbreak that occurred around that time.

SANTA ANNA (ALSO KNOWN AS SANTANA)

It is unclear exactly when this Penateka leader was born, but like Old Owl, he was at the heart of Comanche resistance to Anglo settlement in Texas. According to *Handbook of Texas Online* author Jodye Lynn Dickson Schilz, with Buffalo Hump and Old Owl, Santa Anna raided various Texas settlements such as Linnville and Victoria. Santa Anna was the first Comanche to visit Washington, D.C. When he visited there in December 1846, he was reportedly overwhelmed by the number of whites he saw. Upon returning to his people, he began advocating peace on one hand even as he led raids into Mexico on the other. This caused the Indian agent Robert S. Neighbors to try to stop Santa Anna's raids. He was unsuccessful.

While no one person could stop Santa Anna, disease did. In 1849, he, along with several hundred Penatekas, succumbed to the deadly cholera epidemic that struck them that year.

TEN BEARS

Nearly a dozen Comanche chiefs are pictured on the modern-day cover of the tribal newspaper *Comanche Nation News.* They had such names as Yellowfish, Moway, Horseback, Wildhorse, Big

Looking Glass, Otter Belt, White Wolf, Eschitl, and, of course, Quanah Parker. Ten Bears is also among these.

The actual date of his birth is unclear. Ten Bears is probably best known for his peacemaking efforts between the whites and his people. As he grew to prominence and achieved respect among the Comanche, he ultimately came to be chief of the Yamparika division of the Comanche.

In his efforts to save his people's way of life, he signed two treaties: the Treaty of Fort Atkinson (1853) and the Treaty of the Little Arkansas River (1865). The Treaty of Fort Atkinson was one of a series of agreements in the 1850s between the United States and the Great Plains Indians to ease travel for white settlers going west and to facilitate the building of a transcontinental railroad through Indian lands. The Treaty of the Little Arkansas River created a reservation for the Comanche made up of the entire panhandle of Texas (although the federal government did not yet own it and therefore could not reserve it). Signing these treaties did not mean, however, that he was willing to sacrifice the lives of his people in concession to whites. When Kit Carson attacked warriors fighting the buffalo hunters at the Battle of Adobe Walls in 1864, Ten Bears gathered his warriors, counterattacked, and drove Carson's soldiers away.

Finally, at the historic Medicine Lodge meeting of 1867, Ten Bears spoke to the group assembled there in what was then the largest gathering of tribes and whites. T.R. Fehrenbach's book *Comanches: The Destruction of a People* recounts this speech.

In his words, Ten Bears told the assembly that he did not wish to fight but reminded the whites that they had been the first to "send out the first soldier" and that the Native peoples were simply acting in defense. His speech was recorded and published, and it is still known as one of the greatest examples of oratory. Despite Ten Bears's efforts, including two trips to Washington, D.C., to plead his people's cause, his efforts were in vain. He died in November of 1872 and is buried at Fort Sill Post Cemetery.

QUANAH PARKER

Quanah Parker's mother was the girl who had been taken captive from Fort Parker, Texas—Cynthia Ann Parker. According to his tombstone, he was born in 1852. As he grew, this son of war leader Peta Nokona became quite skilled as a daring raider on the Southern Plains.

When in 1855 the Penateka Band of the Comanche agreed to allow Texas to establish a fort on the Clear Fork of the Brazos River—on the border of the Comancheria—it incensed the rest of the Comanche bands, who stepped up their own raiding. In response, Texas Rangers with the aid of the longtime enemy of the Comanche, the Tonkawa, attacked Comanche villages, indiscriminately killing men, women, and children, even as they slept.

The U.S. government also realized that as long as the buffalo roamed by the millions on the Southern Plains, all Native tribes living there, including the Comanche, would be able to survive. The government allowed, even encouraged, the shooting of buffalo for sport, and buffalo hunters spread like a virus onto the plains. Native hunting groups would come upon a huge herd of dead buffalo, rotting on the plains (often, white hunters would "harvest" only the tongue and hump of the animals as these were considered delicacies by Europeans). The Comanche people were first filled with disbelief, then anger at the indiscriminate killing of the animal that provided so much for them.

In 1860, events took a disastrous turn for the Comanche when they were hunting in Palo Duro Canyon (in what is now north-central Texas, just south of the Oklahoma state line). Peta Nokona, Quanah's father, and most of the men were away from camp, leaving Cynthia Ann (whom they called Naduah) and her daughter, Prairie Flower, or Topsannah, with the women and a handful of warriors.

Quanah Parker's band was the last group to come to the Kiowa-Comanche-Apache Reservation in Indian Territory. Once on the reservation, Parker was named chief of all the Comanche and became one of the wealthiest Native Americans in that era. Pictured is Parker with one of his many wives in 1875.

They were attacked by a band of veteran U.S. soldiers, led by Lawrence "Sul" Ross. The soldiers killed most of the Comanche they found, wounded Peta Nokona, destroyed all the horses, supplies, and shelters they could find—and took Cynthia Ann and her daughter.

Shortly after this, Peta Nokona died from wounds received in battle. Quanah had learned from his father never to trust the white man's words; he had already witnessed treaties broken along with those words. When he grew to adulthood, Quanah became ruthless in his attacks against the ever-encroaching white men.

In 1867, a council of Native American leaders met with whites, supposedly to try to form a kind of alliance. The treaty the white men proposed, however, called the Medicine Lodge Treaty, was for the people of the tribes to give up their native lands and go to a reservation. Quanah and his Quahadi band (which means "antelope") rejected this treaty.

THE RED RIVER WAR

Even after many of the Comanche were moved onto reservation lands in Oklahoma along with the Kiowa and Apache, Quanah refused to go to this restrictive environment, and he continued in his efforts to protect and preserve his homeland. Quanah's daring inspired his Quahadi band to fight every onslaught of the Comancheria made by settlers and U.S. government soldiers. The Quahadi attacked cavalry troops time and time again, following their movements as the soldiers themselves were trying to attack and arrest these warriors.

For decades, Quanah and the Quahadi successfully eluded government soldiers. Stories of their defiant acts only served to inspire those Comanche living on the reservation and made them hopeful of regaining their independence and homelands. The U.S. government knew something had to happen to stop Quanah and his raids once and for all.

One soldier in particular, Colonel Ranald S. Mackenzie, was determined that he and his men would round up Quanah and his

Scene of the Red River War, 1874–1875

Fort Lyon
Fort Larned
Kansas

Dodge City

Arkansas R.

Colorado Territory

Public Land
North Canadian R.
Camp Supply
CHEYENNE-ARAPAHO RESERVATION
Indian Territory

Fort Union
Price
South Canadian R.
Miles
Wichita R.
Darlington Agency
☐ Fort Reno

Adobe Walls
Anadarko ▲

New Mexico Territory
Palo Duro Canyon
☐ Wichita Agency
■ Fort Sill (agency and army post)

Prairie Dog Town Fork

Pecos R.
S T A K E D
Double Mountain Fork
White R.
P L A I N
Buell
KIOWA-COMANCHE RESERVATION
Red R.

Mountain Fork
■ Fort Richardson

Troop movements
▲ Indian village
■ Fort
☐ Agency
✸ Battle
Mackenzie
Fort Griffin

Texas
Brazos R.

0 — 150 miles
0 — 150 km

N

■ Fort Concho

© Infobase Publishing

By 1874, violence and unrest on the reservations of the Southern Plains had begun to worry the U.S. government. The Red River War was the last effort of resistance against the U.S. government staged by the Comanche, Kiowa, and Southern Cheyenne. This map shows the routes taken by the four military units sent by General Philip Sheridan to attack American Indians hiding at Palo Duro Canyon.

band and bring them to the reservation at Fort Sill. The Quahadi called him "Three Fingers," because Mackenzie had lost one of his digits in a battle during the Civil War.

Despite Mackenzie's efforts, Quanah continued in his fight against the U.S. Cavalry, going so far as to stampede buffalo through Mackenzie's camp as he and his soldiers slept. In one raid against Mackenzie and his men, Quanah's party even managed to get close enough to the U.S. colonel to shoot an arrow into him (Mackenzie survived). The Quahadi also raided the camp another night, stealing as many as six dozen horses and a thousand head of cattle. In a rage, Mackenzie sent out a pursuit party, which was attacked by the Quahadi who were waiting in ambush. The pursuit party was led by Lieutenant Robert Carter.

Carter later wrote a description of Quanah as he led the ambush, which has been recounted in Claire Wilson's book *Quanah Parker: Comanche Chief*. Carter wrote an enthralling account of Quanah Parker charging, as he rode a "coal-black racing pony," with a "six-shooter in the air," and his face with a "satanic look" of "brutal joy." This was the first description of Quanah Parker in battle and must have stirred the imaginations of everyone who read it. Carter and most of his men survived the ambush when Mackenzie and his men came to their aid.

After pursuing Quanah and his band for more than 500 miles (805 km) and with foul weather upon them, Mackenzie was obliged to concede defeat and return to Fort Richardson, but the freedom that the Quahadi had managed to retain would not last much longer. In 1874, Comanche warriors, along with some Cheyenne, Kiowa, and Arapaho, began to attack buffalo hunters. Their anger began to spill over and led them to attack whites indiscriminately, wherever and whomever they were. Trading posts, ranches, and wagon trains were all fair game to the Comanche and their allies, who knew that this was a last attempt to save their land, families, and way of life.

Finally, starving and with no other recourse, the warriors and their families turned themselves in to the reservation officials. It was June 2, 1875, when Quanah led his small, dispirited band of warriors, their families, and their wounded to surrender at Fort Sill. Colonel Mackenzie had offered Quanah and his people fair treatment if they gave up and submitted to reservation life. Quanah was wary, but he accepted, because most of the Comanche left in his band consisted of women, children, and the elderly. It was there that, learning of his mother's death, he adopted her last name as his own.

General William Tecumseh Sherman—the man who led the Union army in its brutal and infamous "March to the Sea" during the Civil War—had not become softer or gentler with time. He remained cruel and ruthless, and he wanted some of these "rebellious" people to serve as examples to others. He had 25 of the Comanche and Kiowa warriors arrested and sent in shackles to a prison in Florida. Surprisingly, Quanah Parker was not one of these chosen to be an example to others. Still, his life was about to take a turn no one could have foreseen.

Quanah Parker and his people were not given the fair treatment promised by Mackenzie, but Quanah managed to find ways to help his people not only survive, but thrive. He quickly came to realize that unless his people came to learn and adapt to the white man's ways, they would perish.

He went to live with his deceased mother's people, staying with his uncle Silas Parker, brother to Cynthia Ann. With his white relations, Quanah learned all he could about their culture—their language, how to farm, and other things his people would need to know to thrive in the white man's world. He learned not only English but also Spanish, supported education on the reservation, and even had his children go to the schools there.

He rose to prominence in this strange new world, embracing most of its tenets. So much was Quanah admired by the people he had recently fought against that he was appointed chief judge of a three-man Court of Indian Offenses and made deputy sheriff of Lawton, Oklahoma. He turned into quite a savvy businessman and helped his people become more prosperous by leasing their tribal lands to cattlemen for grazing lands. He also became known for his diplomacy in dealing with Comanche-white issues.

He built a large 12-room house for himself and his family. When he realized that U.S. Army generals wore stars on their uniforms, he placed on the roof four large stars, so anyone who came

Pictured is the massive home that Quanah Parker built on the reservation, which he called Star House. Parker later had stars painted on the roof to mimic those on the uniforms of U.S. soldiers. Behind the house was a tipi that Parker used for sleeping, relaxing, and entertaining visitors. Today, tourists can visit Star House in Cache, Oklahoma.

to the "Star House" would realize that Quanah, too, was someone with whom to be reckoned. Quanah's home eventually became known by everyone as the Comanche White House. In 1905, the man who for decades had fought against the U.S. government rode in Theodore Roosevelt's inaugural parade along with four other chiefs (including Geronimo).

There were some ways of the Comanche that Quanah never forsook, however. He refused to give up any of his seven wives or to cut his long braids; and he founded the Native American Church, a cornerstone of which is the use of peyote in rituals.

Other honors came to be bestowed on this warrior turned diplomat. The town of Quanah, Texas, was named after him

Author Interview with Nick Mejia, Great-Grandson of Quanah Parker

Nick Mejia is a great-grandson of Quanah Parker. Although he was born after his great-grandfather died, Quanah lived on through tales told to Nick by many of his older relatives. Nick also endured the hardships of boarding-school life on the reservation at Fort Sill. Now retired from the railroad business, Nick Mejia is an avid powwow attendee and often emcees as well. He is a living example of what it means to be proud of one's Comanche heritage.

I learned about Quanah Parker as soon as I was old enough to understand language. He was chosen by the U.S. government to be the only chief of the Comanche people because they knew he was smart, and they [U.S. government] needed to have one person in charge, and they picked him to be that person. They knew he could be someone to reckon with because he had outsmarted thousands of soldiers and had surrendered and come into the fort on his own. He was also half-white.

All the old people I listened to, especially as a kid, told me stories about Quanah Parker. He was the most influential leader we ever had. He brought schools in, established land leasing, and set up a tribal justice system, which is still in existence. I think today, if it hadn't been for him, the Comanche would still exist but on a different level; the government would have taken everything had it not been for Quanah Parker. Other tribes are still today fighting tooth and nail to get federal recognition. Due to his tenaciousness, he had the foresight to see way ahead and see that the Comanche would be no more if they continued fighting. He still stands out as a leader of The People. He knew enough to make friends [with whites] quickly and gain insight into

(continues)

(continued)

what whites wanted and needed and gained friendship with cattle barons so they could get grazing rights. He had sense enough to use them [the whites] because he knew they were using the Comanche.

Today, in dealing with the present administration, we must be very watchful, as Quanah was. The state of Oklahoma is fighting to abolish casinos and tribal sovereignty and that's only the beginning. The U.S. government is trying to do away with tribal sovereignty, and we must be aware that no one will do something for tribes without wanting to get something back. Every initiative the government has tried to do for the tribes has failed miserably. Every treaty ever made has yet to be honored by the government.

History has a way of repeating itself. The future remains to be seen, and let us not be overambitious for our people. We must strive for the best as we go into the future.

and he spoke at the town's dedication, blessing the city and its inhabitants.

After struggling with an undiagnosed illness, Quanah Parker died in his beloved Star House on February 23, 1911. In what was at that time the largest funeral procession ever in the history of the state of Oklahoma, Quanah was buried in full regalia befitting a Comanche chief. He lies beside his mother, Cynthia Ann, and his sister, Prairie Flower, in the military cemetery at Fort Sill, Oklahoma. His tombstone reads:

Resting here until day breaks
And shadows fall and darkness disappears
Is Quanah Parker
Last Chief of the Comanche
Born–1852
Died February 23, 1911

Grim Days
for the
Comanche Nation

Those Comanche living in the part of the plains that was first called the Republic of Texas and then, later, the state of Texas, asked for peace with Texans. Texas had just won its independence from Mexico, and the Comanche wanted a clear boundary between how far settlers could go and what their own defined lands would be. They were refused at every turn. Texas politicians stated that wherever white settlers wanted to settle, the Comanche (as well as any other Native Americans, such as the Kiowa) had to leave.

Ignoring the needs of those who were there first merely served to inflame the Comanche people to anger. The result of this was a raid on Fort Parker in May 1836. Fort Parker had been built in 1834 by Elder John Parker in Groesbeck in Limestone County, Texas, near what is now Waco, for protection against Native Americans. Several of the inhabitants of this fort were killed, and some were taken captive. One of those taken was Cynthia Ann Parker, one of the most famous such captives in American history. This has come to be known as the Fort Parker Massacre.

In 1839, the Texas legislature had acquired approximately one million dollars to support citizen militias, which took to seeking out and attacking the Comanche wherever they happened to be. Then Texans turned to betrayal of trust as another weapon against the Comanche.

Part of Native tradition concerns peace talks: When people come together to talk peace, they are to come and go in safety. In March 1840, under the guise of holding a peace conference, Texans invited some Comanche to San Antonio. The Comanche brought with them their wives and children, which for them was the custom, and the women and children waited outside while the "peace talks" progressed.

Instead of peace talks, the Comanche men were surrounded, the doors were locked, and in the ensuing fight, many were killed, including the women and children outside. This came to be called the Council House Massacre and was a major betrayal of trust for the Comanche people and a slap in the face to their cultural values. Worsening the hostilities, later that same year, Texas troops attacked and indiscriminately killed some Comanche people at a place called Plum Creek (between present-day Austin and San Antonio).

So extreme was the resulting hatred between the Comanche and Texas settlers, that even after Texas attained statehood in 1845, the Comanche still made a discernment between "Americans" and "Texans." Peace between the two groups was an off-again, on-again affair, as perennial as the coming and going of the flowers on the plains, which were increasingly being destroyed by the plow and the rail. By the mid-1850s, the U.S. government had established several Indian reservations in Texas, but the settlers' outcry against such close proximity to Native people, especially the "brutal Comanche," was great. So feared were all Native people, in fact, that soldiers began striking preemptively (striking before a threat materializes) against all of them.

A terrible case in point was a massacre of peaceful Cheyenne at Sand Creek, Colorado, by Colonel John Chivington and the Colorado militia in November 1864. Despite the pleas and protests of Chief Black Kettle, who raised both an American flag and a white flag of truce as the 700 soldiers descended upon his encampment of mostly women and children, all except for a handful of survivors were bayoneted or shot during what has become known as the Sand Creek Massacre. This grisly task took the soldiers more than two hours to accomplish. Amazingly, Black Kettle survived.

It did not take long for other Native Americans to get the message. In 1865, the Comanche and Kiowa signed a treaty with

Despite the display of the American flag and the white flag of truce and the promise that Black Kettle's bands would be considered friendly, Colonel John Chivington led an attack that killed an estimated 200 Cheyenne and Arapaho women, elderly men, and children. Above is a depiction of Chivington and his soldiers during the Sand Creek Massacre. Shortly after, the Comanche signed the Treaty of Little Arkansas River.

the United States called the Treaty of the Little Arkansas River, granting those Indian nations the area known as the panhandle of Texas. Again, settlers' cries of outrage were heard by the U.S. government. Two winters later, the government offered the Comanche and Kiowa a "revised" treaty, which settled them into Indian Territory in Oklahoma. What was once land free for the Comanche people to roam became home to the largest single cattle ranch in the history of the West: the XIT Ranch. According to T. Jensen Lacey's book *Amazing Texas*, this area became fenced off with more than 800 miles (1,288 km) of barbed wire, which became such a hated sign of confinement that it earned the moniker "Devil's Rope."

The year 1868 saw a near-repeat performance of troops in their attacks on innocent Native people. That year, Black Kettle and what was left of his tribe were encamped along the Washita River in western Indian territory. Approximately 40 women and children were mercilessly slaughtered, and this time Chief Black Kettle himself was also killed. This charge was led by George Armstrong Custer and his 7th Cavalry. A countercharge was led by a contingent of Comanche, Kiowa, and Arapaho warriors; Custer fled, but his handful of soldiers who had remained to bayonet any survivors met their own grisly fate.

It was about this time in history that one of the most infamous phrases ever to be said was uttered—"the only good Indian is a dead Indian." It happened in 1869, when a Comanche chief named Tochoway, or "Turtle Dove," came to Fort Cobb under the peace flag. This was on the very heels of the massacre of the Cheyenne chief Black Kettle and his entire encampment. Tochoway met with General Philip Sheridan, who was in the area. When Tochoway introduced himself as a "good Indian," Sheridan said something to the effect that the only Indian he'd ever met who was any good was dead. Soon, the phrase "The only good Indian is a dead Indian" was the informal battle cry of soldiers and settlers alike.

DRAWING THE LINE

To protect its settlers from Indian attacks, in 1861, Texas established a line of defense in the form of soldiers camped at 25-mile (40-km) intervals along the frontier. By virtue of such geographical predictability, however, this only served to make it easier for the very attacks the soldiers were in place to prevent. Sometimes, too, the soldiers themselves were the objects of such aggression. In March 1864, Kiowa and Comanche warriors attacked a group of Texas soldiers known as the Frontier Organization. The battle, which took place in what is now Elm Creek in Young County, Texas, resulted in a victory for the Native Americans. Although it was a victory, for the Comanche it marked the beginning of the end, for this merely served to increase the determination of the U.S. government to solve what it called "the Indian problem" once and for all.

In 1864, when Kit Carson attacked Kiowa and Comanche encampments (supposedly to "punish" them for their attacks against settlers in Texas), he was met with extreme resistance. The Kiowa, led by their chief Satanta (or White Bear), joined forces with Quanah Parker.

Historians say one reason U.S. government soldiers were unnerved that day and finally retreated was because of the blaring of a horn they kept hearing. It was not their bugler sounding orders, however. It was Kiowa chief Satanta, who had a horn he used to announce mealtime and was blowing it on the battlefield, confusing the white soldiers.

Students of history must caution themselves against condemning the Native tribes who fought back against the growing influx of white settlers and hunters. In the year 1859 alone, for example, more than 90,000 emigrants traveled the Santa Fe Trail. What was first seen as a small trickle of whites merely passing through the Southern Plains had now become an alarming surge. Even more disturbing to the Comanche, Kiowa, and other Native people living in the area was the fact that many of these people were no

Gold, Greed, and Native Americans in Its Path

On January 24, 1848, a carpenter named James W. Marshall was constructing a sawmill on the American River in northern California. He saw a few glistening flakes in the riverbed and picked them up. The flakes were gold, and news of Marshall's discovery resulted in a flash flood of people traveling from all over, headed to California in search of their fortunes.

Unfortunately for the Native Americans living and making their homes on the Southern Plains, this caused a huge disruption in their lives. Between those traveling through the Native lands and the U.S. government constantly trying to squeeze out indigenous people such as the Comanche, concern turned to dread and dread to dismay, then anger. Retaliation became a necessity rather than a choice—because to choose otherwise was to choose death.

longer "passing through." They were putting down stakes and creating settlements in the grazing and hunting lands so ferociously defended by Native Americans, without regard as to how this would affect the Comanche people's livelihood and even existence.

THE TREATY OF MEDICINE LODGE

In October 1867, in an attempt to settle the "Indian problem" once and for all, Congress sent a commission to negotiate with the tribes of the Southern Plains, including the Comanche. The plan was to persuade the Native people to give up their nomadic ways, settle on land that would be their permanent reservation, and become farmers and ranchers instead of warriors and hunters.

The meeting at Medicine Lodge Creek, a popular location for Sun Dance ceremonies among the plains tribes in what is now southern Kansas, was one of the largest peace negotiations ever seen, with approximately 5,000 members of the southern plains tribes (including the Comanche, Kiowa, Southern Cheyenne, and Southern Arapaho) in attendance. They were met by members of the "peace commission," which included U.S. Army general William Tecumseh Sherman.

In his book, *Comanches: The Destruction of a People*, author T.R. Fehrenbach described the meeting at Medicine Lodge Creek. Surrounded by other members of the peace commission, and in the presence of reporters for various newspapers and magazines, Sherman told the tribal representatives that they must give up their nomadic ways—that resistance was not only futile but would result in their annihilation. He told them that trying to stop the incursion of white settlers into the Southern Plains was analogous to trying to stop the sun and the moon, and all the Native American people should submit to the inevitable.

At the meeting at Medicine Lodge, Kiowa chief Satanta spoke for both his people and the Comanche, saying he did not want the prairie to become red with blood (from battling the white soldiers). Neither, however, did he want to give up the freedom enjoyed by both his people and the Comanche.

For his eloquence in this meeting, Satanta earned the name "Orator of the Plains" by reporters who heard his carefully rehearsed speech, but his words fell on deaf ears. The fate of the Native Americans of the plains, it seemed, had already been decided. Comanche chief Ten Bears also spoke with great eloquence. His speech impressed the reporters covering the historic meeting to the extent that his words were published. This, too, however, could not turn the tide of fate.

Many of the tribal representatives signed the Medicine Lodge Treaty, but those who did not do so thought the treaty would not apply to them since they did not agree with it. They were wrong.

The treaty basically stated that in exchange for submitting and moving onto the reservation (in what is now Oklahoma), they could still hunt in their old hunting grounds in the region that is now southern Kansas and northern Texas. Also, the U.S. government would supply the Comanche and Kiowa people with food and supplies.

Those who submitted to the treaty stipulations were bitterly disappointed. The supplies were meager at best, and even the meat, often rancid, was insufficient. In anger, some young hunters struck out to find wild game—but many of the buffalo herds had been wiped out by white hunters who often killed the animals merely for sport.

In desperation, many of the young men slipped away from the reservation land. It was all they could stand, seeing their women and young children crying in hunger and cold due to the meager rations and supplies given them by the U.S. government. Comanche warriors rode into Texas from their reservation in Oklahoma and raided settlements, seeking horses, guns, and food for their families.

In 1871—four years after the Treaty of Medicine Lodge—desperate Comanche and Kiowa warriors attacked a wagon train headed for Fort Richardson, Texas. They killed seven people on the wagon train and took all they could carry on horseback.

Afterward, the agent in charge of the reservation at Fort Sill, Lawrie Tatum, learned about the incident through talking with the Kiowa chiefs who was responsible for the raid. One of them, Chief Satanta, admitted what he had done but said it was out of desperation.

This was reported to General Sherman, and Satanta and two other Kiowa chiefs were arrested to stand trial for murder. Sherman wanted the chiefs to be hanged, as a warning and example to the other Kiowa and Comanche people, but pro-Indian groups in the East protested this harsh treatment. The Bureau of Indian Affairs (BIA) in Washington, D.C., agreed that the judgment should be less harsh; since their raid was an act of war, the killings would, therefore, not be defined as cold-blooded murder. The three were set free. Sherman then suspended the part of the treaty allowing Native hunters to go on forays, saying that anyone who did so would be shot.

The situation became even worse for the Comanche people. By 1873, due to a new tanning process that could turn hides into leather, the price for a buffalo hide skyrocketed, and hunters shot the bison by the millions. In 1874, in one shipment alone, one firm (Rath & Wright of Dodge City, Kansas) reported a shipment of hides going by rail numbered more than 40,000.

THE BATTLES OF ADOBE WALLS

Adobe Walls was a place in what is now Hutchinson County, Texas. Especially in the mid- to late-1800s, it was important to indigenous people and to the white buffalo hunters and settlers. The area itself was a crossroads for Native people, such as the Apache, Kiowa, and Comanche, and a place where they could hunt buffalo or let their horses graze. It was also, however, too close for comfort for settlers traveling the Santa Fe Trail. Since it was such a crossroads, the crossroads began to be used as a trading post, with only a tipi marking the spot for such activity, but not all indigenous people were open to such transactions with whites. In 1848, whites led by Kit Carson attempted to make the area a permanent settlement, but they were met with predictable resistance by Jicarilla Apache and Comanche warriors.

When Carson came again to Adobe Walls on November 26, 1864, he arrived better prepared. With him were 400 troops, Ute and Jicarilla allies, and two howitzers. There were approximately 5,000 Kiowa-Apache, Comanche, and Kiowa encamped in the area when the attack came. Chiefs Dohasan, Satanta, and Little Bear led their warriors in counterattacks. When it was over, Carson had suffered 3 dead and 25 wounded; the Native casualties numbered more than 100. While this was a major victory for the U.S. government, the Native people would continue to resist white incursion for another decade.

The final, decisive battle of Adobe Walls was June 27, 1874. By this time, Adobe Walls had grown into a true settlement, with a complex including two stores, a corral, a saloon, and a black-smith shop. Comanche chief Quanah Parker led his 700 warriors in another attack of the complex, with the help of the Cheyenne and Kiowa. They were encouraged by a shaman, or medicine man, by the name of Isa-tai, but after about a half day of fighting, the Native warriors retreated, as more and more white buffalo hunters came to the aid of their allies.

When it was over, the army took the bodies of the Comanche warriors they had killed, decapitated them, and impaled their heads on stakes of the corral, to serve as an example of what happened when Comanche and other Native Americans tried to resist the inevitable.

Commemorating the sacrifice of the warriors who died at Adobe Walls, there now stands a granite memorial. It reads, in part: "In Memory of the Indian Warriors Who Died in the 2nd Battle of Adobe Walls." This particular battle is said to be the largest engagement ever, before or since, between U.S. troops and American Indians on the Southern Plains.

THE DAWES ACT

In 1882, Senator Henry L. Dawes of Massachusetts presented a petition to the U.S. Senate. This petition contained more than 100,000 signatures and demanded an improved education policy for Native Americans and an establishment of clear land allotments. In 1887, Congress passed the Dawes Act, granting Native Americans land allotment and citizenship.

Many whites, especially those in sympathy toward Native Americans and their plight, considered this legislation a positive step. For Native Americans, including the Comanche, however, it meant forced boarding school for their children and individual ownership of land. These were contrary to their communal way of living and teaching their children, as well as the way they communed with nature and the land.

In Lawrence C. Kelly's book, *Federal Indian Policy*, he states that the Comanche people resisted the Dawes Act with more determination than other Native nations, mainly due to the land stipulation: One of the terms of the act allowed that, after the land allotments were given to each (male) tribal member, any "surplus" lands could be sold to whites. Kelly states that the Comanche were the most adamant against allotment, since they realized that the act was passed because of pressure from "land-hungry white constituents." The Comanche fought allotment until a U.S. government commission, led by David H. Jerome, presented them with another agreement.

THE JEROME AGREEMENT

In 1892, the U.S. government negotiated a new "treaty," which turned out to be yet another disaster for the Comanche and their related tribes. They were offered the Jerome Agreement, which further reduced the Comanche, Kiowa, and Apache reservation to 480,000 acres (194,256 hectares). For all children born after the Jerome Agreement, there would be new allotments of land, but the remaining land from the previous Medicine Lodge Treaty was opened to white settlement (basically, the U.S. government broke the first treaty in order to create another treaty). The Jerome Agreement did not do any favors for Native Americans, but it did open the way for the Oklahoma Land Rush.

THE OKLAHOMA LAND RUSH

The Homestead Act of 1862, although 30 years ahead of the Jerome Agreement, would change the face of the plains, from the Dakotas to Texas, forever. Combined with the Jerome Agreement, suddenly the Southern Plains were simply there for the taking.

The Oklahoma Land Rush of 1893 saw more than 100,000 white settlers, at the firing of a cannon, race to tracts of land to which they could lay claim. This sealed the fate of many Native Americans, including the Comanche, who had made their lives and homes on the plains. Many who had not surrendered by this time did so. The Comanche were especially devastated when,

The Homestead Act of 1862, the Jerome Agreement, and the construction of the railroad into the western territories over the next 40 years would open vast amounts of land. The release of 270 million acres (10.9 million hectares) of federal land to the public would cause a wave of western settlement that forever changed the prairie from the Dakotas to Texas.

between 1893 and 1901, thousands of whites illegally seized more reservation land. The Dawes Act and the Jerome Agreement were supposed to make the Comanche people's lives better, but instead they got worse.

BOARDING SCHOOL AND RELIGION

Once on the reservation at Fort Sill, Oklahoma, Comanche children were forcibly removed from their families and put into boarding schools. It was reasoned that if they could be put into an environment in which they could be immersed in "white" culture, they could be more quickly and easily assimilated.

At Fort Sill Indian Boarding School, Comanche children were forced to wear the clothing white children wore at the time; their hair was cut and they were not allowed to speak their Native tongue or practice their faith. Doing either often resulted in being beaten by their teachers. This treatment dealt an emotional and spiritual blow to the young Comanche boys and girls, who had been born into a close-knit and interdependent society and who were suddenly thrust into one that favored isolationism and independence. At a time in their lives when they were trying to determine their identities, they were told that being and acting Comanche were bad things, and the only way they could have a good life was to become more like white children.

Clyde Ellis, author of the book *To Change Them Forever: Indian Education at the Rainy Mountain Boarding School*, wrote about the purpose behind boarding schools. This, he wrote, was part of the plan to assimilate all Native Americans into "Anglo" (white) society by forcing Indian children to attend the schools and to prevent them from, in his words, "returning to the blanket," or going back to their Comanche ways.

Suddenly children and teenagers who had before only known the closeness and security of Comanche family life were thrust into an alien and forbidding world. The stark reality of an indoor classroom, stern school administrators, loneliness, and a feeling of not belonging to either white or Comanche culture were all a bitter brew for generations of boarding-school children. For some, this trial by fire hardened them for the even more difficult times to come. For others, they would return to their people as leaders. For all, it marked the final end of their happy days with their families. Many of the Indian boarding schools eventually were closed, the disastrous result of a social and political experiment (Fort Sill Indian Boarding School closed in 1970).

The U.S. government called this "assimilation," and for Native Americans it remains one of the saddest words in the language. One way the Comanche tried to deal with this blow to their culture was through the use of peyote in religious ceremonies.

THE PEYOTE RELIGION

The peyote religion came about relatively late in Comanche history. It was handed down from a tribe in Mexico and made popular in the 1880s by the last formal Comanche chief, Quanah Parker. It is said that the first peyote society was begun in 1890 by a man named John Wilson. His organization was known as the Big Moon Society, which included peyote in its ceremonies.

Peyote is the narcotic fruit of a type of cactus; the peyote cactus bears small buttons that contain the hallucinogen mescaline, but the buttons also contain alkaloids called hordenine and tyramine, which are natural antibiotics. Both the harvesting and use of peyote are surrounded by ceremony.

The consumption of peyote in ritualistic ceremonies ultimately gave rise to the founding of the Native American Church. Ingesting the peyote brought on a feeling of peace; it was also said to induce hallucinations. The Comanche regarded these as something more like the visions they sought, and they embraced peyote as a part of their new religion.

In later days, various Bureau of Indian Affairs agents tried to stop the practice of peyote ceremonies, but Quanah negotiated with them by agreeing to send his children to the reservation school in exchange for the keeping of the peyote practice.

Fast-forward to more recent days. In 1999, the Supreme Court ruled that individual states could outlaw the peyote ceremony and other religious ceremonies. This was viewed with dismay among many Native Americans, who felt it was a setback to the First Amendment, which protects freedom of religion. Two Native American authors, Huston Smith and Reuben Snake, wrote a book to protest this ruling being made by one culture against another.

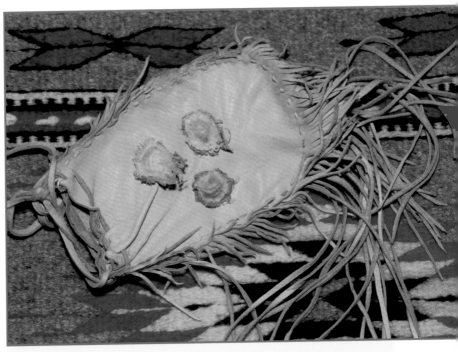

Peyote is used by Native Americans for its healing purposes and also for its hallucinogenic effect during religious ceremonies. For some chapters of the Native American Church, the peyote ritual includes prayer, the eating of peyote, peyote songs, water rituals, and contemplation. Pictured are peyote buttons on a bag.

In their book *One Nation Under God: The Triumph of the Native American Church*, they wrote that "peyote is regarded as a gift from the creator. It counters the craving for alcohol. . . . It is not taken to induce visions or hallucinogenic experiences but because it heals and teaches righteousness."

Many Comanche healers also have used peyote in ministering to the sick. One such healer and shaman (or spiritual leader) was known as Sanapia. She reported using the cactus button in many forms (dried and powdered, made into a relish, or raw) to heal a great number of illnesses ranging from fever to colds, pneumonia, arthritis, headaches, and as a sedative. Others say that peyote helps people work out problems. One of the more well-known Comanche leaders of today, LaDonna Harris, said this in a personal interview: "I teach classes on Comanche. I tell people the rationale for the use of peyote is that we were looking for answers to our questions about life—especially after the white people came."

The modern-day Native American Church still uses peyote in its ceremonies; it is in fact part of the fall celebration the Comanche people celebrate. Today, hundreds of thousands of people are members of the Native American Church, and a "Peyote Meeting" is part of the annual Comanche Nation Fair held in Lawton, Oklahoma, every September.

THE SUN DANCE AND THE GHOST DANCE

Many people believe that all Plains Indians practiced the same religious traditions, but this is not true. Historically practiced by many other Native American nations such as the Blackfeet and Ute, for example, the Comanche rarely held their own Sun Dance (some records indicate it was only done once or twice). When threatened with extinction, however, many Comanche people did embrace the Ghost Dance, initially the vision of a Paiute shaman named Wovoka. The Comanche people were told that if they lived the traditional ways of old and practiced the Ghost Dance, their ancestors would return, along with the great bison herds. Further, Wovoka said, the whites would leave. According to LaDonna Harris, some Comanche practiced the Ghost Dance out of desperation. In December 1890, however, was the time of a terrible tragedy in Native American history. At a place called Wounded Knee, South Dakota, soldiers killed nearly 200 Lakota Sioux who had also embraced the Ghost Dance; most of the dead were the old and sick along with women and children. Where it may not have attracted some Comanche before, peyote became the new religion. New religious practices, however sincere they might have been, were not enough to save the Comanche from surrender to U.S. soldiers.

SURRENDER AT FORT SILL AND RELOCATION

As mentioned earlier in this chapter, once the Comanche people surrendered to federal authorities at Fort Sill, their lives as they had known them were over. With the Dawes Act and the Jerome Agreement, their lands were allotted individually, and the government took the rest (called "surplus") to sell to non-Indians. The four bands of Comanche that were intact settled in the area of Lawton, Oklahoma. Oklahoma itself attained statehood in 1907, and the push for more land for settlers resulted in more Comanche people being tricked out of their tribal allotments.

The years 1900 to 1936 were grim ones indeed for the Comanche. With their meager allotments of land, they struggled to farm and were often obliged to work as laborers for more prosperous white farmers. The drought that resulted in the Oklahoma Dust Bowl seemed to be the final blow to the people still surviving in these trying times. Many people, including non-Indians, began to see that the Comanche's dreadful situation needed to be changed.

In 1928, a survey committee, led by Lewis Meriam of the Institute for Government Research (Brookings Institution), reported on the "failed policies" of the U.S. government as they applied to Native Americans on reservations in 26 states, including the Comanche. It specifically criticized boarding schools for failing to assimilate the young and ignoring the cultural needs of Native American youth. The issues brought up by Meriam's survey still exist: Comanche educator John Tippeconnic III wrote in the Winter 2000 issue of *Journal of American Indian Education* that education is still a challenge. "We are still talking about the problems in Indian education . . . that were identified in 1928," he wrote. The Meriam Report, as it came to be called, was said to be the forerunner of the Indian Reorganization Act.

After Franklin Roosevelt took office in 1933, he signed into law the Indian Reorganization Act of 1934, which also was called the "Indian New Deal." This legislation had three basic tenets. The first principle focused on lands: It returned all lands not already sold to whites, it extended the time the lands would be held in trust from the previous 25 years to indefinitely, and it set aside money with which to buy lands back from whites that had been sold to them unethically.

Second, the indigenous nations were granted limited self-government. The third tenet stated that qualified Native American people were to be appointed to a variety of offices within the Bureau of Indian Affairs, and promising young students would be offered loans to further their educations.

At first, this so-called Indian New Deal was not stipulated for the Comanche and other Native Americans living in Oklahoma, as some legislators argued that the needs of indigenous people living there were covered through other means. Wiser heads, however, prevailed in this argument, and the next year the Oklahoma Indian Welfare Act was passed. It provided those Native people in the state with the same "deal" as those elsewhere—in other words, this offered the Comanche and other Native Americans in Oklahoma the same tenets in the Indian New Deal.

Despite some of these changes, which were seen by many Comanche to be positive ones, there remained a pervasive prejudice across the nation against Native Americans, including the Comanche. During the 1940s and into the 1960s, this double standard was referred to by some as a kind of American cold war, similar to the relationship between the United States and Russia. Dr. Paul Rosier's article "They Are Ancestral Homelands: Race, Place, and Politics in Cold War Native America, 1945–1961" quoted a Moscow (Russia) radio broadcast of 1958 that declared American Indians to be "the most underprivileged people in the United States" and compared reservations to "huge concentration camps."

In a feeble attempt to change Native American stature in relation to "mainstream" America, the U.S. government began a program called "relocation," which offered Native people, including the Comanche, a chance to leave their reservations and receive job training in the cities. The government had not counted on one thing: isolation. Many Native people, longing for home and family, dropped out of the program. For others who stayed with the program, as soon as they got a job for which they had been trained, they were dropped from the relocation program, with no further governmental support. The government called this "termination," which grew out of the attempt to relocate Native American people in the 1940s and 1950s. Termination had its own problems. Without a social safety net and ongoing social services, Native people wound up isolated from their own people, barely eking out a living, surviving in the poorest and most dangerous parts of cities.

Despite the efforts to make positive social and political changes for the Comanche and other Native people, some began to chafe at the slowness with which the federal government was moving to help further their cause and allay their plight. Then it seemed there was an answer to many spoken and unspoken prayers: The era of the 1960s, bringing with it the civil-rights movement, burst upon the United States, and with it, more changes were to come for the Comanche people and others.

The Comanche People in the Mid-twentieth Century

After the grim period of 1900 to 1934, the 1940s through the 1960s were not much better for the Comanche people. Comanche men and women served honorably and well in both World War I and II, seeing this as a way to earn honor for themselves and their tribe through heroic deeds in battle.

The civil-rights movement of the 1960s seemed to pave the way and motivate Native Americans to take action and work to improve their own conditions. The firm, nonviolent political attitude of civil-rights activists such as Martin Luther King Jr. must have been an inspiration to many Native Americans.

For too long, the Comanche and other Native Americans had suffered glaring injustices, loss of culture and pride, and betrayal at the hands of the U.S. government. The path was cleared for an era of Native American activism and resurgence of pride in Comanche identity.

TWENTIETH-CENTURY WARRIORS:
THE CODE TALKERS OF WORLD WAR II

Although they were considered outsiders by the government, Native Americans have served the United States during wartime. Despite the fact that Native Americans were not granted U.S. citizenship until 1924, an estimated 12,000 Native Americans volunteered for military service during World War I. Patty Loew, a television journalist and an associate professor at the University of Wisconsin-Madison, says that "some chose to serve in guard units for a steady income, but many others were motivated by tribal values of obligation, service and protection." Loew, whose Ojibwe grandfather served in all seven major battles of World War I, produced a one-hour PBS documentary chronicling the war stories of Native American soldiers from World War I to Vietnam.

Comanche code talkers during World War II used their Native language to prevent enemies from being able to decipher intercepted messages. This picture of the U.S. Army's 4th Signal Company is on display in a case near the Pentagon's Hall of Heroes.

It is an ironic point of pride that Native Americans often have helped to sustain America in her times of trial. Without the Comanche warriors and their tribal allies, World War II might not have been won by the Allied Forces.

The 2002 movie *Wind Talkers*, about the Navajo code talkers, failed to acknowledge that Comanche Marines also served in this capacity. The day after Pearl Harbor was attacked—December 8, 1941—the United States declared war on Japan. As U.S. forces were engaged throughout the Pacific, they made slow progress toward Japan, due to the enemy's ability to intercept and break coded military messages as they were transmitted. This not only slowed U.S. progress, but soldiers by the thousands were needlessly being killed. The United States recruited Comanche and Navajo men to aid in thwarting Japanese efforts—by transmitting messages via radio and Morse code, but in their own tongue. These messages might have been to guide battleship bombardments on Japanese positions or other important strategies. This language could not be "broken" or decoded by the Japanese, the Germans, or others who were fighting against the Allied Forces. With the aid of these indecipherable messages, America and her allies won the war.

In 1989, these brave soldiers were awarded the Chevalier de l'Order National du Mérite, a great honor bestowed upon them by a grateful French nation. One of the Comanche code talkers of World War II was Charles Chibitty, who received the Knowlton Award in the Pentagon Hall of Fame in November 1999. In September 2003, the Comanche Indian Veterans' Association placed a monument at the Comanche Nation Complex in Lawton, Oklahoma, commemorating the achievement of the 14 heroic code talkers. In June 2005, the association members added a plaque to the monument, which has a description of the code talkers' heroism during World War II. The code talkers were further honored with an exhibit titled "Native Words, Native Warriors," which opened September 25, 2008, at the Comanche National Museum and Cultural Center. Chibitty himself spent his final years traveling the country and telling others of his code-talker experiences until he "walked the Spirit Road" in 2009.

Pictured is the late Comanche Charles Chibitty, a code talker in the U.S. Army's 4th Signal Company. In 1999, at age 78, he received the Knowltown Award at the Pentagon's Hall of Heroes for his service during World War II.

Today, Comanche people—both women and men—serve the United States in uniforms of all kinds. They can be found in the Coast Guard, National Guard, Air Force, Navy, Army, or Marines. They also serve their cities in other uniforms—as firefighters, police officers, and airline security agents.

Incidentally, one might wonder how the Comanche came up with words not normally in their tribal vocabulary, such as "tank" or "machine gun." The Comanche code talkers used their word for "turtle" for "tank" and "sewing machine" for "machine gun." The sound of the sewing machine, they reasoned, was quite similar to that of the machine gun.

The irony is not lost on anyone who studies history—that, once beaten in boarding schools for speaking their Native tongue, these brave soldiers were honored for speaking it, in order to save their homeland in time of war.

RED POWER

It was in the 1960s that the cry "Red Power" began to be heard among the Comanche and other indigenous people. Many of the younger Native Americans were dissatisfied with the slow pace of the federal government in its efforts to correct injustices done over several hundred years. They took matters into their own impatient hands.

These young Native Americans, many of whom were college educated, had a taste of dissent in this Vietnam War era. The American Indian Movement (AIM), founded in Minnesota in 1968, advocated activism in the extreme. They reasoned that symbolic occupation of federal properties would raise U.S. and international awareness of the plight of the Native American people.

The Taking of Alcatraz

On November 10, 1969, Native Americans seized Alcatraz Island in San Francisco Bay. Established as a prison in 1934, the compound built on the 12-acre (5-ha) island had been closed since

1963 due to erosion and structural decline caused by salt water. What began with a handful of Native Americans seizing the tiny island became a focal point for indigenous protest. With some saying "Alcatraz is not an island, sovereignty is the goal," more and more Native Americans began arriving on the island any way they could get there (the Coast Guard attempted a blockade, but some bay residents, captains, and crew assisted those who wanted to get to the island). The taking of Alcatraz, a symbolic gesture, sparked international controversy over the United States' treatment of its indigenous peoples and finally brought attention to their collective plight.

The media embedded with the Native Americans on Alcatraz made non-Indians aware of their indigenous counterparts and their social issues. At the time, unemployment on the reservations was a whopping 75 percent. The suicide rate was 10 times the national average. Depression and alcoholism were also rampant— twin mongrels snapping at Native heels.

According to the Public Broadcasting System (PBS), which aired stories of various Native people during the 19-month-long occupation, more than 100 tribes were represented on this island, which was suddenly a symbol of Red Power and Native pride.

Norren and Meade Chibathi, Comanche Indians from Fort Sill, Oklahoma, were two of these. While on the island, they taught American Indian music and dance to the children and others who had either forgotten or never learned their tribal roots and Native traditions. Alcatraz became, for many people, the first time they had been surrounded by other Native American people. On that island in the middle of foggy, chilly San Francisco Bay, the people experienced the unexpected: cultural renewal and an exhilarating sense of Native pride they had never known before.

The occupation of Alcatraz ended on June 11, 1971. The people were out of fresh water and were obliged to leave. What stayed with many of them—and with mainstream America—was a renewed

From November 20, 1969, to June 11, 1971, the group Indians of All Tribes seized Alcatraz Island and demanded reparations for land that had been taken away from Native Americans. The occupation of Alcatraz has been defined as a key achievement in indigenous civil rights. Above, American Indians celebrated Thanksgiving buffet-style with turkey and trimmings sent over to the island by sympathetic restaurants.

sense of purpose. Native people saw themselves as people with rights—like every other American.

There were some groups, such as AIM, that committed other, more aggressive acts against the U.S. government. Marching into Washington, D.C., they raided the offices of the Bureau of Indian Affairs, destroying files and creating havoc. Following this, they seized the ship *Mayflower II* as it lay at anchor in Plymouth Harbor, Massachusetts.

According to author Dr. Paul Rosier, both sides—the U.S. government and the AIM members—"were using violence, aggression and criminal acts" against each other. When AIM members occupied the site of the massacre at Wounded Knee, on what is now the Pine Ridge Lakota Sioux Reservation, the first occupation ended when federal agents moved in to forcibly remove them, resulting in the deaths of two of the AIM members.

When in 1975 AIM occupied the Pine Ridge Reservation a second time, the results were much more deadly for both sides. This time, the conflict ended only after two federal agents were dead. In the eyes of the U.S. government, AIM leaders were now criminals, and at least one of them, Leonard Peltier, is still in prison. (Rosier states, "Leonard Peltier is in prison but there is a lot of evidence he was framed. Furthermore, the federal government prosecuted AIM leaders using falsified evidence.") Since then, AIM has reorganized and employs peaceful, legal protests to find ways to create change by working with the system rather than against it.

Law and Politics of the Comanche People Today

Most people think of the Comanche as they do many other indigenous tribes: still living in tipis, fighting with the bow and arrow and lance, and not a part of mainstream American history. The fact is that Native Americans often challenge that they are *more* American, not less, than non-Indians. Many Native Americans further contend that they are all distinctly different from other Native nations. As Comanche LaDonna Harris said in a personal interview, "We all [different tribes] are as different from each other as the Chinese are from the English. We continue to celebrate our differences."

The Comanche are not only alive and well in today's world, but despite challenges such as racism and poverty, many are thriving. The improvements begun in the 1930s in Washington, D.C., have continued to gain momentum. In 1990, Congress founded the Indian Arts and Crafts Board to help better the economic conditions of Native Americans by helping them to showcase and sell their handicrafts. Now under the auspices of the U.S. Department of the Interior, the Indian Arts and Crafts Board administers a number of museums with gift shops showcasing handmade wares of indigenous people. Another purpose for the board is to enforce the Indian Arts and Crafts Act of 1990, which provides criminal and civil penalties for anyone selling or advertising products as "Indian-made" when they are not.

WHERE THEY ARE

Although Comanche people are scattered around the globe, their land is in and around Lawton, Oklahoma. Approximately 14,500 people are listed on the Comanche rolls, but according to the Enrollment Office staff, that number is increasing all the time. The tribal headquarters is located in Medicine Park, north of Fort Sill, Oklahoma. While many Comanche people live on their lands in Oklahoma, there are large concentrations of Comanche in Texas, California, New Mexico, and other western states.

Now, in the early part of the twenty-first century, positive winds of change are blowing for the Comanche Nation and its people. With the visionary influence of non-Indians, and due to the perseverance of the Comanche people, they are making great strides toward achieving myriad goals, both personal and tribal.

There are many Comanche people who have been and are shining the way for their people. Some are entertainers, some are politicians, and others are educators. Here are just some of the leaders who have emerged since the 1950s.

LaDonna Harris

Born in 1931 and raised near Walters, Oklahoma, the woman who has been called "The First Lady of Indian Country" was formerly married to Oklahoma senator Fred R. Harris. LaDonna Harris is the founder and president of Americans for Indian Opportunity. A

Comanche activist LaDonna Harris (*right*) is the founder of several organizations that work to assist the Native American population and has been appointed by several U.S. presidents in leadership positions. Here she is pictured with Chilean indigenous leader Clara Bulnes at a ceremony celebrating the approval of the U.N. Declaration of Indigenous Peoples' Rights in Tiwanaku, Bolivia.

political activist herself, Harris has served on scores of federal government committees concerned with issues pertinent to women and Native Americans. Harris is the role model for what an effective activist is—someone who knows how to use the system to invoke change. She has written an autobiography, *LaDonna Harris: A Comanche Life*, and has been the subject of a book (with Wilma Mankiller, former chief of the Cherokee Nation) by author Sarah Eppler Janda called *Beloved Women: The Political Lives of LaDonna Harris and Wilma Mankiller*. Author Janda asserts that, in a time when minorities were fighting for recognition and for their rights, Harris and Mankiller forged a niche for women in politics.

One of the many recent achievements for which Harris is best known is the Ambassador's Program. Begun in 1992 through Americans for Indian Opportunity, the program recruits promising young Native Americans, ages 25 to 35, and trains them to be a voice among indigenous peoples.

The documentary video on the Americans for Indian Opportunity, posted on its Web site, was created by Julianna Brannun (also Comanche). The video, titled *LaDonna Harris: Indian 101*, says that Harris has raised national awareness and with her vision has become a leader. While some activists have only stirred up resentment and anger against the U.S. government, Harris's work continues to instigate action. She has also inspired her children: Her daughter, Laura Harris, is the executive director of AIO; another daughter, Kathryn Harris-Tijerine, is an adviser with AIO.

Wallace Coffey

Great-grandson of the famous orator Ten Bears (who gave an eloquent speech at the Treaty of Medicine Lodge), Wallace Coffey was educated at Harvard but returned to Comanche country to help his people. In an interview with the online magazine *Pow-Wow Oklahoma!*, he was quoted as saying, "I have a Harvard degree and an Indian education—what more can you ask for?"

True to his values, he holds that education is the way for his people to make progress in today's world, while continuing to cherish the old traditions of the Comanche people. Coffey served the Comanche people well as chairman for years, having first been elected in 1991. In April 2009, he stepped down and was replaced by Michael Burgess, who will be up for reelection in 2012. Coffey continues to serve as master of ceremony at powwows, something he has enjoyed for years.

Kevin Gover

Being of both Pawnee and Comanche descent, Gover's career has been impressive. Gover grew up in Oklahoma. After receiving his bachelor's degree from Princeton University and his law degree from the University of New Mexico, he joined the faculty at the Sandra Day O'Connor College of Law, located at Arizona State University. While there, he served on the university's Indian Legal Program and has taught courses in American Indian policy. Appointed by President Bill Clinton in 1997, Gover served that administration as assistant secretary for Indian affairs in the U.S. Department of the Interior, a position he held until 2000. Gover is currently director of the Smithsonian Institution's National Museum of the American Indian, located in Washington, D.C.

MODERN-DAY ISSUES

In the 1960s, the United States government adopted new policies and programs in a widespread effort to address some of the social ills affecting the country. As part of the "War on Poverty," the Office of Economic Opportunity launched government-funded legal services programs throughout the nation to provide legal representation to the disadvantaged. Some of those programs were set up on or near Indian reservations and large Indian communities. The people running the programs came to realize that the legal problems of their Indian clients were, for the most part, governed and

Kevin Gover, an educator and laywer, has been called a "briefcase warrior." He is a member of the Pawnee and Comanche tribes. Today, Gover oversees the largest museum dedicated to the life of Native peoples in the Western Hemisphere, the Smithsonian Institution National Museum of the American Indian.

controlled by a little-known area of law—"Indian law"—that was driven by treaties, court decisions, federal statutes, regulations, and administrative rulings. They also found that few attorneys outside of the legal services system were willing to represent Indians, and those who did generally worked on a contingency basis, only handling cases with anticipated monetary settlements. Very few cases were handled on contingency, meaning many issues would not get to court.

During this same period, the Ford Foundation, which had already assisted in the development of the NAACP Legal Defense

Fund and the Mexican American Legal Defense Fund, began meeting with California Indian Legal Services (CILS) to discuss the possibility of creating a similar project dedicated to serving all of the nation's indigenous people. CILS had already established somewhat of a reputation for taking on Indian legal cases. As a result of those meetings, the Ford Foundation awarded CILS a planning grant in 1970 and start-up funding to launch the Native American Rights Fund (NARF) in 1971.

As a pilot project of CILS in 1970, NARF attorneys traveled throughout the country to find out firsthand from the Indian communities what the legal issues were. They also began a search for a permanent location for the project, which was initially being housed at CILS's main office in Berkeley, California. The site needed to be centrally located and not associated with any tribe. In 1971, NARF selected its new home and relocated to Boulder, Colorado.

An 11-member all-Indian steering committee (now a 13-member board of directors) was selected by the CILS Board of Trustees to govern the fund's activities. One of these was Comanche chairman Wallace Coffey. Individuals were chosen (as they continue to be today) based on their involvement with and knowledge of Indian affairs and issues, as well as their tribal affiliation, to ensure a comprehensive geographical representation.

NARF continued to grow at a rapid pace over the next several years. In 1971, the project incorporated in the District of Columbia and opened its first regional office in Washington, D.C. An office close to the center of government would prove critical in future interaction with Congress and federal administrative agencies. The Carnegie Corporation of New York awarded NARF start-up funding in 1972 for the creation of the National Indian Law Library, a national repository for Indian legal materials and resources. More than 10 years later, in 1984, NARF established its second branch office in Anchorage, Alaska, to take on the Alaska Natives' issues of tribal sovereignty, land claims, and subsistence hunting and fishing rights.

The Tribal Supreme Court Project

Today, many of the battles in Indian country are being fought in the courtroom. Many judges who lack an understanding of the fundamental principles underlying federal Indian law and are unfamiliar with the practical challenges facing tribal governments are making decisions that threaten the continued sovereign existence of Indian tribes. Perhaps the greatest threat to Indian tribes comes from the recent decisions of the U.S. Supreme Court. As noted Indian law scholar David Getches found, in the past two decades, Indian tribes have lost approximately 80 percent of their cases before the Supreme Court. In his article, *Beyond Indian Law: The Rehnquist Court's Pursuit of States' Rights, Color Blind Justice and Mainstream Values*, Getches provides an in-depth analysis of the court's rewriting of Indian law and how that has resulted in losses to sovereign Indian nations. And these losses have been severe. The court has in recent years taken a very aggressive approach to eroding tribal sovereignty and jurisdiction. At the same time, the court has been increasing state jurisdiction over reservations.

In 2001, tribal leaders formed the Tribal Supreme Court Project as a part of the Tribal Sovereignty Protection Initiative. The project was created to coordinate resources, improve strategy, and strengthen Indian advocacy before the court. The project operates under the theory that if Indian tribes take a strong, consistent, coordinated approach before the U.S. Supreme Court, they will be able to reverse, or at least reduce, the erosion of tribal sovereignty and tribal jurisdiction by the federal courts. The Tribal Supreme Court Project is jointly staffed by attorneys from the NARF and the National Congress of American Indians (NCAI).

Comanche Jimmy Arterberry, who is in charge of historic preservation for the Comanche Nation, said this in a telephone interview: "All Indian tribes, including the Comanche, are and will be affected by NARF and the Tribal Supreme Court Project's actions. In this, we are unified."

The Native American Graves Protection and Repatriation Act (NAGPRA)

As Europeans settled in this continent, a kind of double standard regarding the dead and their artifacts came into being. Strict laws were laid down regarding the graves and burial sites of Anglos, while Native American remains and burial sites were there for the taking, often in the name of scientific research.

NARF staff attorney Walter Echo-Hawk and his historian brother, Roger, set out to change the laws regarding the protection of Native American bodies and burial sites. Their work resulted in a new legislative act, which now protects such remains and artifacts by law.

Archaeologists and museum curators want unlimited usage rights to the skeletal remains of Native Americans, while indigenous groups believe no remains are to be excavated and all materials already on exhibition should be returned to Native groups for reburial. Above are skeletal remains from Islands Field Site, an Indian burial ground in Delaware.

Known as the Native American Graves Protection and Repatriation Act (NAGPRA), the bill was signed into law in 1990 by President George H.W. Bush. The significance of this law spoke volumes to all Native American people. As Walter Echo-Hawk wrote in *Battlefields and Burial Grounds: The Indian Struggle to Protect Ancestral Graves in the United States*, "For the first time, government recognized that Indian remains were human beings, not 'archeological resources.'"

Comanche Jimmy Arterberry, who is in charge of repatriation of Comanche remains and artifacts for the tribe, remarked, "The Comanche Nation has been very active in applying the [act], as there are numerous remains being held in repositories around the country." He went on to say that other countries, such as England, continue to hold human Comanche remains in their museum repositories and that the work to get them returned to the Comanche people is an ongoing one. Arterberry said that all repatriations are an emotional experience, but one exceptionally emotionally charged repatriation had to do with retrieving a Comanche child's head, which until 2000 was held by the Mabee-Gerrer Museum of Art in Shawnee, Oklahoma. "The museum curator," he wrote in an e-mail, "was resistant to our claim and even at the eleventh hour [believed] the museum had a right to the child."

Casinos: Helping Education

Like virtually all state governments across the country, the Comanche government has supported gaming enterprises in order to raise much-needed funds for social services. The Indian Gaming Regulatory Act, which was enacted by Congress in 1988, gave power to all Native nations to establish gaming facilities. The Comanche Nation established its own Tribal Gaming Commission in December 2005. The purpose of establishing gaming facilities is to both strengthen Comanche self-government and ensure and promote tribal economic independence. There are currently four gaming facilities located in and around Lawton: the Comanche Spur, the Comanche Red River, the Comanche Nation Casino, and the Comanche Star. According to officials at the tribal headquarters, the proceeds from gaming go in part toward Comanche education and for other social services, such as the treatment of domestic violence victims and programs for the elderly.

Walking "The Red Road"

Many Native Americans today will say they were proud to be indigenous when it was not "cool." The truth is, with a reemergence of interest in anything relating to the First People, many are now coming forth saying they are Native American.

Are You Native American? Here's How to Find Out!

In the past—before written birth records and other government documents—people had difficulty tracing their ancestry. Tracing one's Native American roots was even more challenging, as ancestors' names changed so often. Much of people's Native American ancestry was known through stories passed down through the family. Today, people who think they may have Native American ancestry in their background can find out in a rather simple way: through DNA testing.

With the click of a mouse or the dialing of a toll-free number, there are several companies that can ship DNA test kits for testing in the privacy of one's home. Most kits have people obtain a painless scraping in which they take a tissue sample from the inside of their cheek (this tissue is called *mucosa*). The kit is then sent back to the company, with the mucosa safely inside. The lab then performs DNA testing on the sample and sends results to the applicant. It is said that these results reveal genetics that go back as far as 500 years. (See Web sites in the back of this book for more information.)

Sometimes people say they were not open about their Native ancestry because their families kept it a secret. Other times, the person has had his or her DNA tested, to see if they are of Native American descent. At any rate, as the number of recorded indigenous peoples grows, these demographics will surely begin to evoke a change in the political landscape and how all Native people are treated.

The Dawes Act: An Update

A recent case in point occurred in December 2009. For 13 years, 300,000 Native Americans had been in a dispute with the federal government, claiming they had been swindled out of billions of dollars in oil, gas, and timber royalties as decreed by the Interior Department through the Dawes Act of 1887. No one had ever received a penny before 2009, and when the Obama administration settled the dispute, the U.S. government agreed to disperse more than $1.4 billion to the Native American plaintiffs. According to the Comanche Nation Enrollment Office, this legal settlement will "positively affect every enrolled member" of the Comanche Nation. The attorneys with Native American Rights Fund claimed this as a major victory.

As these and other victories are claimed by the Comanche and by other Native Americans, they will continue to move forward— the ones who call themselves "The Numunu," or "The People," will be a viable part of the future.

Culture and Modernism of the Comanche People Today

In many ways, the Comanche people continue to practice traditions inspired by their past. The sweat lodge, for example, is still used today; as in days of old, it is part of a purification ritual. Values such as honesty, bravery, and compassion are still important to the Comanche, but one value that remains paramount is generosity. Giving to others, as in the past, is still a way by which people gain admiration from those around them.

"Giving is a way of life for the community, families and individuals in Native American and indigenous cultures," wrote John E. Echohawk, executive director of the Colorado-based Native American Rights Fund, in a letter to NARF supporters. "Whether the gift is one of words, prayers, time, energy, or love . . . it's considered to be a part of our interconnectedness to one another."

TOURISM: THE NEW ECONOMY

Many people, both non-Native and indigenous, are yearning to explore more of America's history and culture; this includes sites of Native American interest. More people are touring historical sites and attending powwows.

If you ever want to experience Native American celebrations, one of the best places to do this would be in the town of Anadarko, Oklahoma. Called simply the "Fair" by Native Americans in Oklahoma, the American Indian Exposition is held every year in late summer. Representatives from more than 39 nations gather for singing, dancing, and exhibition of costumes and selling of their handiwork. On the heels of this is the *inter-tribal ceremonial* held in Gallup, New Mexico. Non-Indians are always welcome at these celebrations, known as powwows, and they are worth going to despite the intense heat visitors might experience in July in the plains! Many Comanche dancers and talented craftsmen attend powwows held across the country. Called the "powwow circuit," Native American celebrations begin in May and run through September.

There are many other ways to experience and come to appreciate Comanche culture besides powwows. To commemorate the Treaty of Medicine Lodge, you can visit Peace Treaty Park in the city of Medicine Lodge, Kansas. It honors the gathering of Native tribes and whites in the fall of 1867, when the people came together to consider signing the Treaty of Medicine Lodge.

Every three years there is a reenactment of this historic meeting; the most recent one was in October 2009. There is also a huge pageant planned for September 2011 (Kansas's one-hundred-fiftieth anniversary).

The town of Anadarko, Oklahoma, has proclaimed itself as "The Indian Capital of the Nation" and is the largest Native American tourist center in Oklahoma and the United States (the state of Oklahoma has earned the nickname "Native America" and has

During the Medicine Lodge Peace Treaty Pageant, covered wagons make a circle for protection. A pageant reenacting the 1867 peace treaty signing is held in Medicine Lodge, Kansas, every three years.

included this phrase on its automobile license plates). In Anadarko, visitors can tour "Indian City-USA," to gain better understanding of how the Comanche people lived before the incursion of white settlers. Seven southwestern tribes are represented in this outdoor museum—the Kiowa, Comanche, Apache, and Wichita among them—and visitors can explore reproductions of tribal communities. Especially during the summer months, visitors are entertained and enlightened with expositions such as tribal dancing and powwows.

Quanah Parker's famous "Comanche White House," or "Star House," is on private land in the center of Cache, just outside Lawton, Oklahoma. Visitors can see the house if they call ahead. As of press time, the Comanche Nation is attempting to purchase the Star House and to move it to the reservation.

In Carnegie, Oklahoma, visitors can find the Kiowa Tribal Museum, which has many artifacts and items relating to their traditions shared with the Comanche when they ruled the Southern Plains. In Fort Sill in Lawton, there are the graves of many Native people who died in captivity; they lie in an area of the Old Post Cemetery called "Chief's Knoll." Quanah Parker, his mother, Cynthia Ann Parker, and Quanah's sister, Prairie Flower, are all buried together in Fort Sill.

Through the support of Comanche Nation Economic Development, another establishment has been created to encourage understanding between cultures while helping Native people improve their economic lot. That establishment is called "Native Journeys," and it is a travel and tourism project that includes southwest Oklahoma and northern Texas. Native Journeys now works closely with the Oklahoma Tourism and Recreation Department and the Texas Lakes Trail Region (in northern Texas). Native Journeys is also working with the Fort Worth (Texas) Convention and Visitors Bureau to create a Quanah Parker Heritage Trail, which has its beginnings in Texas. One tour is currently called "Lords of the Plains" and is a day trip solely focused on Comanche cultural and historic sites.

In the city of Lawton, Oklahoma, the Comanche National Museum and Cultural Center (CNMCC) has exhibits galore depicting various aspects of Comanche life. One of its most recent efforts was the hosting of a national traveling exhibit titled "50 Years of Powwow," which began in September 2009 and traveled through the country until January 2010. The exhibit honored the four Comanche Powwow Societies (Walters Service Club, Comanche Little Ponies, Comanche War Scouts, and the Comanche Homecoming Committee). The exhibit was conceived and put together by the American Indian Center of Chicago and developed by the Field Museum. It included photographs depicting traditional powwows across the United States. The photographs show drummers, singers, dancers, people/vendors showing and selling

(continues on p. 106)

Dancing, Native American Style

Every August, Gallup, New Mexico, plays host to a massive intertribal ceremony. Above, a Kiowa Comanche performs the fancy dance.

At powwows, visitors will see a variety of tribal dances. For example, there are women's shawl dances, grass dances, and the elaborate fancy dance. The Comanche people are said to be among some of the best fancy dancers in the United States, and every summer they compete with other Native American nations at the American Indian Exposition at Anadarko, Oklahoma.

People who want to learn how to fancy dance first have to master the basic step, called the "fast tap-step," which is a combination of a one-footed tap and a hop. Winners of these dance competitions have practiced this step so much they have been able to add to it, with dramatic turns and jumps.

Many non-Indians believe that the "war dance" was something Native Americans did before going off to battle. This is not true; the war dances had their origins in warriors returning from a battle, victorious. They relived their valor on the battlefield with vigorous bodily movements set in time to the drum. The war dance was therefore a victory dance done after the battle. As in the fancy dance, the Comanche people are extremely proficient in the war dance.

When you go to a powwow, observe the movements of the dance competitors and you will begin to see that there is a pattern to their movements and a symbolism to their costumes and related regalia. A certain etiquette is expected of visitors. One must never, for example, touch any part of a dancer's clothing or regalia, for this is a sign of disrespect. Visitors who wish to photograph dancers or others should get permission first. One part of a powwow in which visitors may participate is a blanket dance, which takes place between dance competitions. The arena director walks in a circle within the powwow arena, carrying a blanket. People are expected to throw money into this blanket as the director walks by. The money usually goes toward travel expenses of the drummers, since they are often uncompensated.

(*continued from p. 103*)
their traditional handicrafts, and other aspects of this Native American traditional celebration. Perhaps most importantly, this exhibit and others like it help non-Indians better understand and relate to their tribal counterparts.

Comanche people also honor their veterans, and tourists are encouraged to take part in these celebrations. Clyde Ellis wrote in the Summer 1999 issue of *The Western Historical Quarterly* of the importance of dance and celebration. The Comanche people, Ellis wrote, hosted a homecoming dance for the Korean veterans. That was in 1952, and since then it has become an annual event, now known as the "Comanche Homecoming."

COMANCHE IN THE ARTS

As in the arena of law and politics, many Comanche are leading the people in the areas of the arts and entertainment as well as sports. Here is just a sampling:

Thomas Edison Ford

Nicknamed "Brownie," this man of Comanche descent rose to become a gravelly-voiced country singer and balladeer. He was born in Gum Springs, Oklahoma, in 1904, and in his youth served as a ranch hand. Later he moved to Baton Rouge, Louisiana, then put down his roots in Caldwell Parish (also in Louisiana). He was an adept storyteller, both in words and music, and this talent resulted in the National Endowment for the Arts giving him the National Heritage Fellowship Award in 1987. In 1995, his album titled *Stories from Mountains, Swamps & Honky Tonks* was released through Flying Fish Records (Chicago), preserving both his voice and his sometimes gritty, often spiritual, tales.

Although he died in August 1996, his music lives on through his albums. He has left an indelible mark on music and also on the people whom he has known. Jerry Moseley of Columbia, Louisiana, performed the eulogy at Ford's funeral. In a phone interview,

Moseley said of Ford, "He was one of a kind—he was humble and you'd never know that he had received awards and had even been invited to the White House—I believe it was during the Clinton administration. He entertained people until his last day; at the age of 92 he was still performing. He was the last of the old-time cowboys."

George "Comanche Boy" Tahdooahnippah

This young, super-middleweight boxer has been undefeated since he began boxing. Of both Comanche and Choctaw descent, at the age of 23 in 2001, the young man first turned toward amateur kickboxing but was so successful at this he decided to try his hand at boxing. Mentored by professional boxer Grady Brewer, Tahdooahnippah won his first professional fight by TKO and, as of press time, is undefeated. He is currently the Native American Boxing Council Champion.

In a telephone interview, Tahdooahnippah commented on his life and his message to young people. "Coming from the struggles of being a Native American," he said, "I think people need to keep on believing and not give up on themselves. People tend to give up [when things are bad] but they need to know to believe in themselves and that they should never stop growing and learning." Tahdooahnippah should know the importance of education: He graduated from Cameron University in May 2010 with a degree in business management.

"Doc Tate" Nevaquaya

Born July 3, 1932, his given name was Joyce Lee Nevaquaya, after Dr. C.W. Joyce, who delivered him. He was given the nickname "Doc" early on, then assumed the name "Tate" when entering Fort Sill Indian School, where a Christian name was required. The name Nevaquaya means "well-dressed" in English.

Nevaquaya was a masterful, self-taught artist and drew world renown for his paintings. As such, in 1986, he was the first Oklahoman to win the National Heritage Fellowship Award; his art was listed among Best Investments for 1987; and he was named a National Living Treasure in 1995 by then-Governor Keating. His talents did not stop there: Nevaquaya began to research Native flute construction and tunes, in order to preserve this part of his culture for future generations. In his flute playing, he also excelled, performing at such venerable institutions as the Kennedy Center in Washington, D.C., in 1982, and New York's Carnegie Hall in 1990. Although he died in 1996, Nevaquaya lives on in his music and art. He also has left a legacy through his four sons—Tim, Calvert, Edmond, and Sonny—all of whom are talented like their father.

RECONNECTING WITH THE SHOSHONE

In recent years, the Comanche have begun hosting a Shoshone reunion. Now an annual event, the first such reunion was held in 2000. Its origins, however, were even earlier than that. In the 1960s, two friends, one Shoshone and one Comanche, began talking about the days gone by, when the two tribes were one. They began talking to others and between themselves about how a reunion might happen to allow the two nations to rekindle a relationship.

Now attended by tens of thousands, the Shoshone reunion is a three-day event. In 2009, it was held in Lawton, Oklahoma, at the Comanche Nation Tribal Complex. Usually held in September, the reunion is open to all—even non-Indians. Some of the events include veterans' recognition, tribal games, basket-weaving demonstrations, a fry bread contest, herbal workshops, flute concerts, and all kinds of dancing.

COMANCHE FLAG AND PATCH

The shape of the Comanche patch is round, symbolizing a war shield. The colors blue and red are symbolic of those colors carried during ceremonies. On the flag patch is a red silhouette of a Comanche on horseback. The weaving line through the center honors their past affiliation with the Shoshone, the name of which means "snake," honoring the past, when the two tribes were one.

LANGUAGE

In days of old, when the Comanche ruled the plains, their language was the common one shared by people—the lingua franca of the plains. When sign language was impossible, people spoke Comanche to one another, even if they were from other Native tribes or were non-Indians.

Today, the speaking of Comanche is realizing a reemergence, as the older and more adept at the tongue teach the youth. On the Comanche reservation, there is now a language immersion program in place. As its name implies, people who want to learn Comanche have access to many books written in Comanche and English, with CDs giving help on pronunciation. The immersion center also welcomes authors' questions if they wish to put Comanche words in books they are writing.

MODERN-DAY WARRIORS

Just as Comanche men and women served honorably in battling enemies, so they continue to serve the U.S. government today in various uniforms. Women in uniform also serve their country in a variety of ways. The first Comanche woman to graduate from West Point was Cadet Jennifer Rae Burns, who graduated in May 2009.

Veterans are honored by their Comanche people in a number of ways. Comanche soldiers returning from service in Iraq and Afghanistan are celebrated for their courage while in the line of fire. The tribal newspaper, *Comanche Nation News*, has a regular column honoring all veterans, "Comanches in Uniform."

Lanny Asepermy of Apache, Oklahoma, is in charge of the Comanche Veterans' history. In a telephone interview in January 2010, he gave these numbers: "During World War I," he said, "we had 58 Comanche involved in the conflict. In World War II, that number was 186. There were 136 of us in the Korean War, and in Vietnam, 286 Comanche fought." He added that "the Persian Gulf conflict saw 33 Comanche soldiers, and today, there are 46 fighting in Iraq and Afghanistan." Asepermy added that these numbers might sound low, but given the small population of the Comanche Nation, it is significantly higher than the number of non-Indian soldiers: "One out of every thousand Americans served [in war]," he said, "while ninety out of every thousand Comanche served; we have a service rate ninety times higher than the national standard."

Asepermy also said that even before World War I, Comanche served the U.S. military. "Comanche served in the cavalry between 1876 and 1884, then again in 1892 to 1897. There were 976 Comanche who served during those years; they were scouts for the U.S. Army." Asepermy added, "We lost the warrior status when we were placed on the reservation, then got it back in 1892. We say it's not just about being a warrior; we serve in the military because this is our land. We lost our land once and we don't want to lose it a second time." Asepermy himself is a Vietnam veteran; he served in the U.S. Army from 1966 to 1990 and retired as a sergeant major. He also was one of Charles Chibitty's pallbearers (the last of the Comanche code talkers).

TECHNOLOGY: THE COMANCHE LEAD THE WAY

Some Comanche are warriors in other places besides on the battlefield: They fight to save lives from natural disasters and are using technology to do so. One example of this is in the realm of weather research. Don Burgess is a research scientist with the Cooperative Institute for Mesoscale Meteorological Studies based at the National Weather Center in Norman, Oklahoma. Burgess is a true "storm chaser," of the type made popular in the 1996 movie *Twister*. He heads up a special project named "Verification on Rotation in Tornadoes Experiment 2," referred to as Vortex 2 or V2 for short. Burgess participated in the original Vortex study in 1994, the purpose of which was to research in detail the origin and evolution of tornadoes. His research is truly lifesaving, as it has led to greater advance warning of deadly tornadoes. He hopes his research will ultimately lead to accurate forecasts of where and when tornadoes will appear, so people can get out of harm's way.

PRESERVING TRIBAL CULTURE: SIA

One of the sources of conflict between modern-day Native Americans and the U.S. government has related to the ceremonial use of feathers of endangered animals. Some administrations have been

The eagle is sacred to many Native American tribes. Some consider them messengers between gods and humans, others see them as signs of fertility or peace, while others use their feathers to welcome important guests. In this picture, a young bald eagle is released during an American Indian celebration.

more understanding of the importance of feathers in ceremonial use and have not sought to prosecute those who use feathers in this way. For example, the Clinton administration issued an order stating that any "Native American in possession of feathers is untouchable, unless that possession is suspect."

Since then, Comanche William "Billy" Voelker established "Sia," the Comanche word for "feather," to work with the U.S. Fish and Wildlife Service to preserve and protect federally recognized feathers and birds. Historically, Native Americans have revered such birds as the hawk and the eagle; this has come in conflict with the laws of the U.S. government. Sia was established to bridge the legal gap between Native Americans' rights and what the law requires. Voelker has grown up with an interest in birds and wildlife. Voelker, whose middle name is TwoRaven, learned the value of protecting wildlife and preserving his Native culture at his grandmother's knee. It seemed a natural outcome of his upbringing to establish Sia.

Sia has done more than simply work with the U.S. government. It is the first organization in the world to reproduce bald eagles through artificial insemination and has released more eagles into the wild than any other group in the world. Sia has noted that around the globe in zoos and other such facilities, these endangered birds molt on a regular basis, and Native Americans should have access to these feathers. Sia is working on ways to legally accept such feathers through a salvage program, to be able to use these feathers in ceremonies. One caveat of the law is that, while Native Americans are exempt from prosecution for possession of such feathers, they must not make any money from using the feathers. According to Voelker, "They must not benefit monetarily from the use of protected bird parts."

Sia was begun through the Comanche Ethno-Ornithological Initiative, and it is now affiliated with the international Eagle Conservation Alliance.

EDUCATING AND PRESERVING CULTURE

The Comanche Nation College was founded in August 2002 through tribal charter. This was done with the authority of the Comanche Nation Business Committee and General Council. The Comanche Nation College was the first tribal college established in Oklahoma; its students are educated in a culturally rich atmosphere. According to President Consuelo Lopez's statement on the college's Web site, its approach is best described as "ancient moccasins on modern feet." A two-year college, the CNC has a partnership with Cameron University.

People of the Comanche Nation continue to revere the past, but they also honor the future by preparing for that future and whatever it brings. As Quanah Parker's great-grandson Nick Mejia said, "We must remember the past and make sure that the mistakes of the past do not repeat themselves. We must be alert and ready to take on whatever the future brings and honor our ancestors as we move forward into this modern world."

Chronology

1520	Spanish explorers arrive in the New World (present-day United States). They bring the horse with them.
1600s to early 1700s	Shoshone and Comanche part ways; the Shoshone go to the northwest and the Comanche establish the Comancheria.
1700s	Comanche acquire horses and become equine masters.
1720s	Comanche begin trading with French traders.

Timeline

1600s-early 1700s

Shoshone and Comanche part ways; the Shoshone go to the northwest and the Comanche establish the Comancheria.

1830

The Indian Removal Act is passed by Congress.

1867

Comanche trust lands are established by the Treaty of Medicine Lodge Creek

1600 — 1800

1700s

Comanche acquire horses and become equine masters.

1849

The discovery of gold in California results in throngs of people coming through the Comancheria.

1887–1906

Tribal lands are divided into allotments through passage of the Allotment Act of 1887.

1779	In a "peacemaking attack," Don Juan Bautista de Anza with his Spanish soldiers, along with Ute and Apache warriors, kill a band of Comanche, including war chief Green Horn.
1786	Spain and the Comanche agree to a truce.
1803	The Louisiana Purchase opens western lands to settlers and homesteaders.
1830	The Indian Removal Act is passed by Congress.
1836	Texas wins its independence from Mexico; more settlers come to the area.
1845	Texas gains statehood; more settlers arrive.
1849	The discovery of gold in California results in throngs of people coming through the Comancheria.

1990

The Native American Graves Protection and Repatriation Act is passed, protecting sacred sites, burial grounds, and artifacts belonging to Native Americans.

1907

Most of the Comancheria becomes part of Oklahoma, which attains statehood.

1900   2000

2009

The Obama administration settles a dispute over the Dawes Act of 1887; it will distribute $1.4 billion to more than 300,000 tribal members in compensation for royalties owed them since that time.

1971

Native Americans take over Alcatraz; they occupy the island and former prison site for 19 months.

1865	The Civil War ends; the federal government steps up its actions against Native people and sends more troops in the land of the Comanche as well as other Native people on the plains.
1867	Comanche trust lands are established by the Treaty of Medicine Lodge Creek.
1874	The Battle of Adobe Walls, one of the largest battles between U.S. soldiers and Native Americans, is fought between a U.S. expeditionary force and Kiowa and Comanche warriors.
1875	Quanah Parker and his remaining band of Quahadi Comanche are one of the last to come to the reservation in southwestern Indian territory at Fort Sill, Oklahoma.
1880s	Quanah Parker becomes principal chief of the Comanche; he negotiates with Texas ranchers, offering them grazing leases.
1887–1906	Tribal lands are divided into allotments through passage of the Allotment (Dawes) Act of 1887.
1892	The Jerome Agreement is passed, amending items in the Allotment Act.
1907	Most of the Comancheria becomes part of Oklahoma, which attains statehood.
1911	Quanah Parker "walks the Spirit Road" and is buried in Fort Sill.
1935	Oklahoma Indian Welfare Act is passed by Congress.
1940s	The U.S. government begins terminating aid to many Native Americans.
1966	The Comanche write their own constitution and form a tribal council and the Comanche Business Committee.
1970s	The Native American Rights Fund is founded in Boulder, Colorado.
1971	Native Americans take over Alcatraz; they occupy the island and former prison site for 19 months.

1990   The Native American Graves Protection and Repatriation Act is passed, protecting sacred sites, burial grounds, and artifacts belonging to Native Americans.

2002   The Comanche Nation College is established in Lawton, Oklahoma.

2009   The Obama administration settles a dispute over the Dawes Act of 1887; it will distribute $1.4 billion to more than 300,000 tribal members in compensation for royalties owed them since that time.

Glossary

ΫΫΫΫΫΫΫΫΫ

agent   A person appointed by the Bureau of Indian Affairs to supervise U.S. government programs on a reservation or in a specific region.

anthropologist   A scientist who studies human beings and their culture.

archaeologist   A scientist who studies the material remains of past human cultures.

band   A loosely organized group of people bound together by the need for food and defense, by family ties, and other common interests.

Bureau of Indian Affairs (BIA)   A federal government agency, now within the Department of the Interior, founded to manage relations with Native American tribes.

Comancheria   The Spanish word for the area on which the Comanche people lived. The Comancheria was located on what are now parts of present-day Colorado, Oklahoma, Kansas, and Texas.

coyote   An animal common in Comanche folktales; often a mischievous being.

culture   The learned behavior of humans; socially taught activities; the way of life of a people.

Curtis Act   A federal law that placed Native Americans completely under the control of the U.S. government. The law was used to force the Comanche into white culture and forbade them from practicing their traditions and speaking their Native tongue.

Dawes Act   In 1887, this legislation (also known as the Allotment Act) was to give an allotment of land to each male Comanche, in addition to other promises.

Ghost Dance   A dance, which emerged in 1890 inspired by a Paiute shaman called Wovoka. Some Comanche practiced it for a time. Living like a traditional Comanche and dancing the Ghost Dance would eventually restore the plains, including the buffalo herds, and drive away the whites, according to Wovoka.

Indian Reorganization Act (IRA) It repealed the Dawes Act and appropriated funds for higher education for promising Native students.

Llano Estacado The Spanish term for the expanse of plains along most of the New Mexico–Texas border.

regalia Special clothing or accessories; finery indicative of an office or membership.

repatriation The returning and reburial of human remains, funerary objects, and other artifacts.

reservation Land set aside for Native use.

shaman A spiritual leader.

treaty A legal and binding document by which two opposing parties make an agreement.

tribe A society consisting of separate communities united by culture, family ties, religion, and other things.

vision quest A four-day fast, usually performed by the young, during which they were alone. Their vision would be their personal "medicine," or guardian.

Bibliography

Auster, Bruce B. "A Leaf from Leif: Columbus Might Have Been a Viking Disciple," U.S. News Online. Available online. URL: http://www.usnews.com/usnews/doubleissue/mysteries/columbus.htm.

Brandon, William. *Indians.* Boston: Houghton Mifflin and Company, 1989.

Branum, Julianna. "LaDonna Harris: Indian 101." (video) Americans for Indian Opportunity. Available online. URL: http://www.aio.org/aio_gallery/video.

Cantor, George. *North American Indian Landmarks: A Traveler's Guide.* London: Visible Ink Press, 1993.

Claiborne, Robert. *The Emergence of Man: The First Americans.* New York: Time-Life Books, 1973.

"Comanche Nation." The Comanche Language and Cultural Preservation Committee. Available online. URL: http://www.comanchelanguage.org/.

Comanche Nation News, Lawton, Okla. Accessed various articles. Also interviewed various Comanche staff members and the editor.

Deloria, Phillip J., et al. *The Native Americans: An Illustrated History.* Atlanta: Turner Publishing, Inc., 1993.

Echo-Hawk, Roger C., and Walter R. Echo-Hawk. *Battlefields and Burial Grounds: The Indian Struggle to Protect Ancestral Graves in the United States.* Minneapolis: Lerner Publications Co., 1994.

Fehrenbach, T.R. *Comanches: The Destruction of a People.* New York: Da Capo Press, 1994.

Freedman, Russell. *Indian Chiefs.* New York: Holiday House, 1987.

Getches, David H. "Beyond Indian Law: The Rehnquist Court's Pursuit of States' Rights, Color-Blind Justice, and Mainstream Values," 86 *Minnesota Law Review* (2001).

Goodin, Barbara. "A Comanche History." Snowwowl.com. Available online. URL: http://www.snowwowl.com/peoplecomanche.html.

Green, Rayna. *Women in American Indian Society.* New York: Chelsea House Publishers, 1992.

Hamalainen, Pekka. *The Comanche Empire*. New Haven and London, Conn.: Yale University Press, 2008.

Heinemann, Sue. *Amazing Women in American History: A Book of Answers for Kids*. New York: John Wiley & Sons, Inc., 1998.

Jones, David E. *Sanapia: Comanche Medicine Woman*. Prospect Heights, Ill.: Waveland Press, Inc., 1984.

Kelly, Lawrence C. *Federal Indian Policy*. New York: Chelsea House Publishers, 1990.

"Kevin Gover, Director National Museum of the American Indian," Smithsonian Institution Online Newsdesk. Available online. URL: http://newsdesk.si.edu/admin/bios/gover.htm.

Lacey, T. Jensen. *Amazing Texas*. Chattanooga, Tenn: Jefferson Press, 2008.

———. *The Blackfeet*. New York: Chelsea House, 2005.

Lodge, Sally. *The Comanche*. Vero Beach, Fla.: Rourke Publications, Inc., 1992.

Mails, Thomas E. *The Mystic Warriors of the Plains*. New York: Doubleday & Co., Inc., 1972.

———. *Plains Indians: Dog Soldiers, Bear Men and Buffalo Women*. New York: Bonanzo Books, 1973.

Matthiessen, Peter. *Indian Country*. New York: Viking Press, 1984.

Meadows, William C. *The Comanche Code Talkers of World War II*. Austin: The University of Texas Press, 2003.

Melody, Michael E. *The Apache*. New York: Chelsea House Publishers, 1988.

Mooney, Martin J. *The Comanche Indians*. New York: Chelsea House Publishing, 1993.

Nies, Judith. *Native American History: A Chronology of a Culture's Vast Achievements and Their Links to World Events*. New York: Ballantine Books, 1996.

Niethammer, Carolyn. *Daughters of the Earth: The Lives and Legends of American Indian Women*. New York: Collier Books, 1977.

Penn, Michael. "Professor's Film on Native American Soldiers to Air on PBS," *University of Wisconsin-Madison News*. Available online. URL: http://www.news.wisc.edu/14317.

Powers, William K. *Indian Dancing and Costumes*. New York: G.P. Putnam's Sons, 1966.

Schilz, Jodye Lynn Dickson. "Santa Anna." *The Handbook of Texas Online*. Available online. URL: http://www.tshaonline.org/handbook/online/articles/SS/fsa30.html.

Smith, Huston, and Reuben Snake. *One Nation Under God: The Triumph of the Native American Church.* Santa Fe, N.M.: Clear Light Press, 1996.

Spencer, Robert F., and Jesse D. Jennings, et al. *The Native Americans.* New York: Harper & Row, Publishers, 1977.

Staeger, Rob. *Native American Religions.* Philadelphia: Mason Crest Publishers, 2003.

"Tribal Supreme Court Project." Native American Rights Fund. Available online. URL: http://www.narf.org/sct/supctproject.html.

"Wallace Coffey," *Pow-Wow Oklahoma!* Available online. URL: http://powwowok.com/pwok-interviews/78-wallace-coffey-p4.

Wallace, Ernest, and E. Adamson Hoebel. *The Comanches: Lords of the South Plains.* Norman, Okla.: University of Oklahoma Press, 1952.

"William Temple Hornaday: Saving the American Bison," Smithsonian Institution Online Archives. Available online. URL: http://siarchives.si.edu/history/exhibits/documents/hornaday.htm.

Williams, Colleen Madonna Flood. *Native American Family Life.* Philadelphia: Mason Crest Publishes, 2003.

Wilson, Claire. *Quanah Parker: Comanche Chief.* New York: Chelsea House Publishing, 1992.

Yacowitz, Caryn. *Comanche Indians.* Chicago: Heinemann Library, 2003.

Author Interviews

Author interview of Jimmy Arterberry, Comanche Historic Preservation and NAGPRA officer. (Interviewed several times between January 10 and January 25, 2010.)

Author interview of LaDonna Harris, Comanche activist and teacher. (Interviewed several dates between September 9, 2009, and January 4, 2010.)

Author interview of Nick Mejia, great-grandson of Quanah Parker. (Interviewed several dates between September 9, 2009, and January 3, 2010.)

Author interview of Ray Ramierez, Native American Rights Fund. (Interviewed November 28, 2009.)

Further Resources

Exley, Jo Ella Powell. *Frontier Blood: The Saga of the Parker Family.* College Station: Texas A&M University Press, 2009.

Fleet, Cameron, ed. *First Nations—Firsthand: A History of 500 Years of Encounter, War & Peace Inspired by the Eyewitnesses.* Edison, N.J.: Chartwell Books, 1997.

Kooper, Philip. *The Smithsonian Book of North American Indians Before the Coming of the Europeans.* Washington, D.C.: Smithsonian Institution Press, 1986.

Lippert, Dorothy L. (Choctaw), and Stephen J. Spignesi. *Native American History for Dummies.* Indianapolis: Wiley Publishing, 2007.

Mann, Charles G. *1491: New Revelations of the Americas Before Columbus.* New York: Alfred A. Knopf, 2005.

Weatherford, Jack. *Native Roots: How the Indians Enriched America.* New York: Fawcett Columbine, 1991.

Wright, Ronald. *Stolen Continents: The "New World" Through Indian Eyes.* Boston: Houghton Mifflin Company, 1992.

Film/DVD

Comanche! (Amazon.com Exclusive, 1956). MGM/United Artists Video, 2001. Director: George Sherman.

Comanche Moon (2008). Sony Pictures. Director: Simon Wincer.

Comanche Warriors (2010). A&E Home Video.

Web Sites

American Indian Education Foundation
http://www.nrcprograms.org

A branch of National Relief Charities, this is a nationally recognized charity that supports Native American students enrolled in post-secondary schools, helping them realize their dreams of achievement through education.

Americans for Indian Opportunity
http://www.AIO.org
Founded by LaDonna Harris, the goal of this organization is to enrich the cultural, political, and economic lives of Native Americans through activism. The site addresses legal issues and news pertaining to international indigenous peoples and offers information about the Ambassadors Program.

The Comanche Language and Cultural Preservation Committee
http://www.comanchelanguage.org/
This comprehensive site offers Comanche history, language immersion, a newsletter, products, and books for sale.

The Comanche Nation of Oklahoma
http://www.comanchenation.com
This is the official site of the Comanche Nation. The site offers all types of information, including community news, educational services, support services, employment opportunities, and tourism information.

Comanche National Museum and Cultural Center
http://www.comanchemuseum.com
The Comanche National Museum, which opened its doors in 2007, educates the public about Comanche history and culture through workshops, exhibits, and teaching programs.

Eagle Conservation Alliance Web Site
http://www.EagleConservationAlliance.org
This Web site includes information and events surrounding Sia.

Genelex DNA testing
http://www.healthanddna.com/
Genelex offers at-home DNA test kits, as well as information about genetics and ancestry.

Indian Country Today
http://www.indiancountrytoday.com/
This award-winning weekly newspaper features the latest news relevant to the indigenous peoples of America.

The Lawton Constitution

http://www.swoknews.com/

Based in Lawton, Oklahoma, this daily newspaper includes news relevant to the Comanche people.

The National Museum of the American Indian

http://www.americanindian.si.edu or http://www.nmai.org

Part of the Smithsonian, the National Museum of the American Indian works to educate the public about Native culture and offers outreach programs for educational enrichment.

Native American Rights Fund

http://www.narf.org

This nonprofit organization provides legal representation and technical assistance to Native Americans.

Snow Owl

http://www.snowwowl.com

This site is dedicated to educating people about the beauty, spirituality, and the current and past issues of Native Americans. The site is comprehensive, offering information on Native American legends, powwows, recipes, and music artists and instruments.

Picture Credits

Index

About the Contributors

ΎΎΎΎΎΎΎΎΎΎΎΎΎ

T. JENSEN LACEY is an author, freelance journalist, photographer, and teacher with a master's degree in education. She has written more than 700 articles for newspapers and magazines and is a contributor to the *Chicken Soup for the Soul books*. Her other book in this set includes *The Blackfeet*. Lacey is of Comanche, Cherokee, and Seneca descent, is a charter member of the National Museum of the American Indian, and a member of Western Writers of America.

Series editor **PAUL C. ROSIER** received his Ph.D. in American history from the University of Rochester in 1998. Dr. Rosier currently serves as associate professor of history at Villanova University (Villanova, Pennsylvania), where he teaches Native American History, American Environmental History, Global Environmental Justice Movements, History of American Capitalism, and World History.

In 2001 the University of Nebraska Press published his first book, *Rebirth of the Blackfeet Nation, 1912–1954*; in 2003, Greenwood Press published *Native American Issues* as part of its Contemporary Ethnic American Issues series. In 2006 he coedited an international volume called *Echoes from the Poisoned Well: Global Memories of Environmental Injustice*. Dr. Rosier has also published articles in the *American Indian Culture and Research Journal,* the *Journal of American Ethnic History,* and *The Journal of American History*. His *Journal of American History* article, titled "They Are Ancestral Homelands: Race, Place, and Politics in Cold War Native America, 1945–1961," was selected for inclusion in *The Ten Best History Essays of 2006–2007*, published by Palgrave MacMillan in 2008; it won the Western History Association's 2007 Arrell Gibson Award for Best Essay on the history of Native Americans. In 2009 Harvard University Press published his latest book, *Serving Their Country: American Indian Politics and Patriotism in the Twentieth Century*.